Here's what the pros say about THE MUCKRAKER'S MANUAL

"THE MUCKRAKER'S MANUAL is one of those exceptional books that way outclass everything else on the subject."
— *CoEvolution Quarterly*

"...AN EXCELLENT GUIDE to the fundamentals of investigative journalism from a radical perspective."
— *Alternative Media*

"THE MUCKRAKER'S MANUAL is another fine Loompanics offer. This book describes the methods used by professional detectives and investigative journalists to get at the truth. Numerous very effective methods are discussed. I consider this book to be of great value to me and all persons with investigative needs."
— *REBEL*

"(THE MUCKRAKERS MANUAL) is by an experienced, no-shit reporter, and his tips and how-to's are hard-earned....If you wanted to write a novel about an investigative reporter, this would be a goldmine."
— *Science Fiction Review*

THE MUCKRAKER'S MANUAL

HOW TO DO YOUR OWN INVESTIGATIVE REPORTING

By M. Harry

Loompanics Unlimited   Port Townsend, WA

THE MUCKRAKER'S MANUAL
© 1980, 1984 by Loompanics Unlimited
All Rights Reserved
Printed in U.S.A.

Published by:
Loompanics Unlimited
P.O. Box 1197
Port Townsend, WA 98368

Cover by Kevin Martin

ISBN: 0-915179-03-2
Library of Congress Catalog Card Number: 84-80233

TABLE OF CONTENTS

Forward: From the Author 11
Chapter 1: Investigative Reporting, Fact & Fiction 14
Chapter 2: What to Look For 25
Chapter 3: Do Your Homework 36
Chapter 4: Developing "Inside" Sources 54
Chapter 5: Documents: Your Gold Mine 59
Chapter 6: Who Are You...When 70
Chapter 7: Interviewing Techniques 73
Chapter 8: Infiltration 79
Chapter 9: Special Sources 91
Chapter 10: Information Analysis 97
Chapter 11: When to Stop an Investigation 111
Chapter 12: Protecting Sources 117
Chapter 13: Can You Prove It? 121
Chapter 14: Do It Electronically 128
Appendix 1: Harry's Laws 132
Appendix 2: Editing for Accuracy 133
Appendix 3: The Citizen Investigator's Library 142
Appendix 4: A Note from the Author 145

FORWARD

From The Author

There are two maxims of investigative reporting that every citizen investigator should take heart from. I'll call them Harry's Laws. *Harry's First Law* is: **There is dirt on everyone.** *Harry's Second Law* is: **Anyone can dig up the dirt on anyone else if they want to badly enough.** Think about it. Every person and organization has done something they don't want other people to know about. Finding out what they've done -- the "dirt" they're hiding -- is the soul of investigative reporting. After you've finished this manual you should know most of the techniques to follow through on Harry's Second Law.

There is, of course, a corollary to Harry's Laws: if you wanted to badly enough, you could find out the real name of the author of this manual hiding behind the pseudonym "M. Harry". Most of my enemies already know. But for those who don't, the pseudonym should make things a little more difficult and expensive. Here are some clues about the person behind M. Harry: I have been a professional journalist for the last 18 years. Most of that time was spent learning how to do, and then doing, investigative reporting. I do not have a college degree -- except the two I bought through the mail for $10. Nor have I ever taken a single journalism class or seminar. Nor do I have any so-called "credentials" (except two mail-order ordination certificates). My only professional asset is a fat scrapbook of the investigative reports I've done.

I have conducted investigations on almost every subject that has ever interested me. These investigations have included published reports on: business secrets; union corruption; the CIA and FBI; different elements of organized crime, including extortion rackets, drug and gun running, arson for profit and illegal alien smuggling; corrupt public officials and political groups; religious institutions; and clandestine radical organizations, both on the political "right" and "left". Along the way, I have also accumulated a wealth of incriminating information on hundreds of people and organizations that has yet to be published. The information I developed on some of my subjects has caused them a lot of trouble -- investigations by the IRS, state attorney generals, postal officials, the Federal Elections

Commission, and a Congressional committee or two. All of the techniques described in this manual are ones that I have actually used, and all of the anecdotes are true.

So here is *Harry's Third Law:* **If Harry can do it, anyone can.**

College degrees and journalism classes are practically useless to the citizen investigator. The difficulties of investigative reporting are vastly over-rated. All that is really involved is some common sense, a dose of stubbornness, and familiarity with the basic information-gathering techniques described in this manual.

Once you have mastered the material in this manual, you will find that your ability to dig out the dirt on people and organizations has many applications that have nothing at all to do with writing. You'll also find that these same techniques can be applied to finding information that is pretty well hidden, but doesn't qualify as "dirt".

In a society that is burying itself in megatons of information daily, the ability to find a particular set of data is rapidly becoming an extremely marketable skill -- witness two careers that were virtually unknown in the public sector until a few years ago: "information manager" and "information analyst".

Aside from these careers you can, if you like, use your investigative skills for: blackmail; propaganda (Harry's First Law of Propaganda: "Start with the facts"); political sabotage; corporate espionage; spying for your own or for a foreign government; getting the kind of "insider" information you can use to make profits on the stock market without gambling; cleaning out the crooks in your local community; or even for personal revenge.

A knack for uncovering hidden facts can be turned into a profitable newsletter operation. As federal laws curtail the information-gathering activities of the FBI and as local regulations restrict police spying, the market for certain kinds of newsletters and news services will be booming.

Your imagination is the only limit to the sources of profit to be found in being able to uncover hidden facts. Investigative reporting for publication, my specialty, is probably the *least* profitable and most competetive of any of the potential markets for investigative skills. But these skills are readily transferable, so after you've made your first fortune in a profitable information market, you can always take the plunge into investigation for publication to gratify your ego or as a public service.

Whether you use the investigative techniques described in the following pages for profit or not, you will, I hope, benefit in one way that is vastly more important than money: *the knowledge that you have the ability to find out anything you want about anyone.* This is a potent source of spiritual and psychological power.

CHAPTER 1
INVESTIGATIVE REPORTING, FACT & FICTION

Ever since Woodward and Bernstein's reportage of Watergate was popularized in their best-selling book and on film, the job of "investigative reporting" has suffered from an excess of glamourization, much like the job of "private investigator" was glamourized by television shows, and spying by James Bond movies. All hoping to be future Woodwards and Bernsteins, droves of young people decided they would make "investigative reporting" their career and entered colleges to take up journalism majors. Unfortunately for most of the graduates, there was a sudden glut of people looking for jobs that didn't exist. Unfortunately for the rest of us, not only did a college degree become mandatory for even the most mundane newspaper job, but a public impression was given that only those people who had gone through years of specialized training could do investigative reporting. And, of course, to be eligible for this training, the prospective investigative reporter would have to meet the criteria for admission to one or another college. These criteria not only included skills totally unrelated to performing investigations, but required a sufficient amount of money to pay for tuition and for survival -- money that could otherwise have gone to support investigative work.

As a result of the identification of investigative reporting with a university degree, some so-called "journalistic ethics" taught in college journalism classes were applied to what was taught as "investigative reporting".

This process was in part responsible for the replacement of the Spencer Tracy image of investigative reporters by a new and impractical mythology. The new mythology, with its emphasis on "objectivity", virtually put an end to the great American tradition of muckraking journalism that had, in the late Nineteenth and early Twentieth Centuries, been responsible for creating a lively press as well as positive social change.

Today's media elite, partly by virtue of their university degrees and "academic sophistication", have given us a sanitized and lifeless press. The large media who have the financial resources to sponsor investigative reporting seldom do. As a result, millions of Americans no longer read the news sections of their daily papers, and even those who do are left without an inkling of the corruption that permeates every public institution they must deal with. The public is therefore shocked by exposes of public corruption and alienated from the political process. Had muckraking managed to survive as a major institution into the last decade, more Americans would function in the *real* world of public affairs rather than in the sanitized and phony world described by much of the contemporary news media.

The best investigative reporting -- and citizens' investigations that may never reach the mass media -- follows in the American muckraking tradition. Its motto is "expose, expose, expose" -- a direct contradiction of so-called journalistic "objectivity" because it is based on the presumption that there *is* something to expose along with the judgement that it is in the public interest to expose the conditions reported.

The investigator begins with the presumption that there is something fishy about his or her subject, develops an hypothesis of what kind of criminal or other illegal or unethical acts the subject might be involved in, carefully constructs a strategy of investigation, and sets out to prove or disprove the hypothesis. That is hardly the kind of "objectivity" that J-school grads espouse on their first months at the job. If the investigator can prove her or his hypothesis about the subject of investigation, the job is done. By contrast, the so-called "objective" reporter is usually limited to simply reporting allegations about a person along with that person's denials and explanations. The investigator collects evidence to build a case much as a police agency, private investigator, or public prosecutor does. If the subject of investigation is contacted at all, it is in the hope that he or she will say something that is self-incriminating.

None of this means that the good investigator does not have ethics, or that certain aptitudes aren't useful in becoming a good investigator. It's simply that the ethics and aptitudes are not those taught in ivory towers -- they are ethics and aptitudes born of pragmatic necessity.

Aptitudes

The most useful aptitudes for the would-be investigator are listed here. If you already have some or all of them, you are well on your way to success.

1) Street sense. Street sense is difficult to describe. It

generally comes along with experiencing tough times. Some of the things that street sense brings with it are:
- The ability to lie and fabricate stories as needed and without being self-conscious
- The ability to sense when other people are putting you on
- A nose for trouble
- A sense of what is a scam and what is a legitimate operation

2) Cynicism, skepticism. You will find it very useful if you are the kind of person who does not believe *anything* until you see it for yourself. And then, if you're smart, you will question what you've seen or heard.

3) Passion. Most of the work of investigation is tedious, and requires a lot of determination. It makes the job a lot easier if you're the kind of person who gets downright angry when someone tries to hide something from you, lies to you, or is involved in activities that you detest. Your anger will give you the motivation you'll need to get the job done. (People on the other side of the investigative coin could take a lesson from this: nothing is more certain to provoke an investigation than trying to cover something up from a reporter or denying him or her information. For example, I once was almost convinced to drop an investigation of an organization called The Conservative Caucus. I even went so far as to ask if I could join. The head of the organization wrote me -- and not too politely -- that I could not join. Two days after this rejection I became a card-carrying member of the Caucus which gave me ample opportunity to develop a serious investigation of the organization. I'm told that to this day the head of the Caucus shudders when he hears my name.)

4) Timidity. I don't know why, but all of the investigative reporters I have met are gutless wonders. It seems to go with the job. (Yes, I'm a gutless wonder as well.)

5) Stubbornness/Flexibility. The good investigator is like certain kinds of radiation -- he or she will allow nothing to interrupt an investigation. Meanwhile, the investigator must be flexible enough to change tactics when it's necessary, and even be able to give up an hypothesis that isn't proving to be correct. It is a curious mix of personality traits, a kind of perfect balance between yang and yin, or if you like, of Missouri mule and Spanish mercury.

Never say "no" to an investigator.

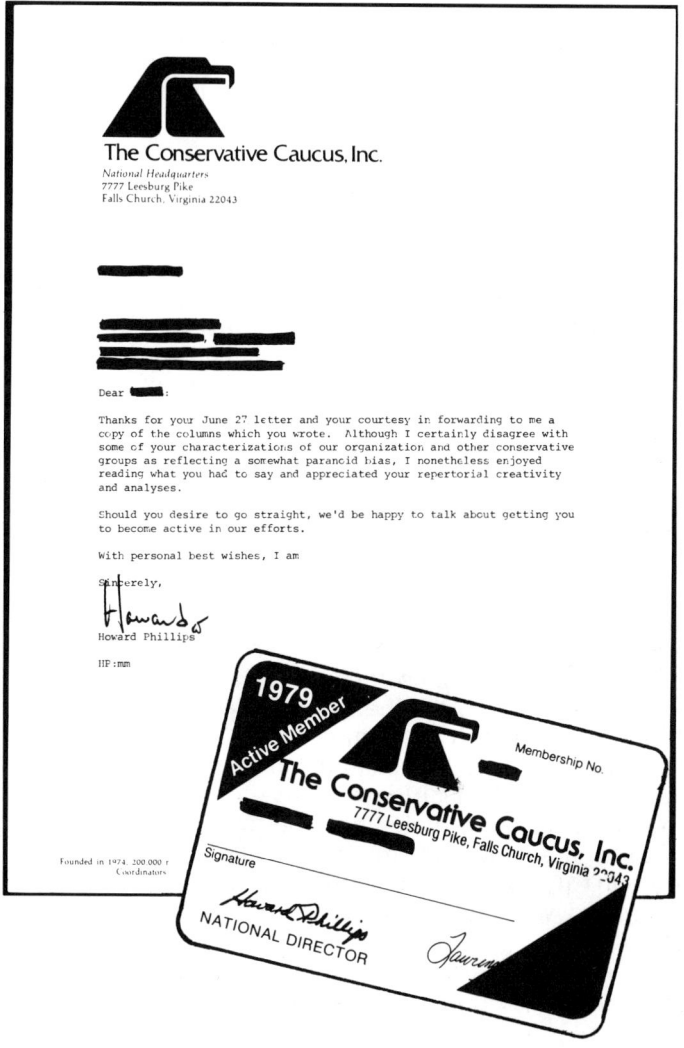

17

Ethics

Even muckrakers and citizen investigators have ethics. In some cases, they even overlap what are "journalistic ethics". The citizen investigator's ethics, however, have little to do with idealism or morality. Rather, they are pragmatic guidelines that function to protect the investigator. Any benefit to the public from these guidelines is incidental. Presumably, the public benefits any time it can learn the truth about people or institutions that affect it. Note that the list includes no mention of "objectivity".

1) Keep it legal. If you can't find the information you want without breaking the law, the information probably isn't worth the trouble. Remember, the object of your investigation is to get the goods on someone else, *not* to land in jail. Generally, as a citizen investigator, you should be able to find out anything you want without having to break the law.

I've known a couple of neophyte investigators who had watched too many detective programs and thought it would be quicker and easier for them if they broke into someone's house to look for evidence, or wanted to open someone's mail. It's a bad idea. Not only may you land in jail, but whatever you do happen to find may turn out to have little or no practical value. Let's say you know there's evidence for your investigation just beyond a locked door and you *do* manage to break in and get it. OK. You have the goods. Now what are you going to do? You've just found evidence proving that your subject is as crooked as a coiled rattler and ought to be sent to the nearest maximum security prison. So you turn your "evidence" over to the police. What happens? The police can't use evidence obtained illegally in court. The chances are that your subject will get off free, sue you, and you will end up behind bars. Of course, if the office door happens to be unlocked and you walk in and happen to see the evidence, that's a different story.

Another temptation that should be resisted is bugging. Same story as for breaking and entering. What good is the information if you can't use it? Of course, no one is saying that you can't walk around wired for sound and record what you hear in a meeting.

If you've built a strong case that shows that your subject is a crook and that even more damning evidence may be found in her or his private possession, then get someone else to do the dirty work for you: the police, who can do it all quite legally.

2) Stick to the facts. Not only will sticking to the facts help you in the event you're sued for libel or slander, *facts* are the only currency of any value to you no matter how you apply your investigative skills. If you get a reputation for dealing in counterfeit goods, not only will your work be discredited, but you're not likely to get much cooperation from good sources in the future. And believe me, your reputation *will* get around. As you will find, there is a kind of underground network of investigative journalists and citizen investigators. Your reputation for integrity can be the key to opening many doors.

This guideline should be followed in its spirit and not just by the letter. For example, in 1978 one Michigan reporter had an interview with Robert Shelton, head of the United Klans of America. He told the reporter that members of his organization would be present to protect their women at a liberal-dominated women's conference. The reporter quoted Shelton and got great headlines in the national media that went something like "KLAN THREATENS DISRUPTION AT WOMEN'S CONFERENCE". The reporter, however, failed to finish Shelton's quote, I later learned. He had explicitly told her, he said, there would be no violence or provocation of violence by his organization.

The competent investigator, however, would have known that someday Shelton might come in handy as a source for other investigations and would have left the propaganda to a professional propagandist.

3) Keep your promises. If your investigation is getting close to uncovering illegal acts, some of your sources may demand that you protect them as part of the deal to give you information you need. If you make such a promise, you had better be prepared to keep it if you expect to continue your career as an investigator. No one forced you to make any promises, so if you make them, keep them. In general it is a good idea to keep your lips sealed if you can. Every so often a person who is just beginning as an investigator will do a lot of bragging about his or her confidential sources. Needless to say, the braggart will have a hard time getting the kind of help he or she needs in the future.

4) Keep an open mind. This may sound contradictory to the investigative goal of building a case to prove an hypothesis about a subject's activities. It may even sound perilously close to "objectivity". But this guideline is double protection for you.

In the first place, it seems like a sure thing that people suing you for libel will be able to ask you questions about your "state of mind" while you were conducting the investigation and compiling your report. As obnoxious as this is, since you may have to put up with such questions anyway, why not be able to honestly say you had an "open mind", rather than a mind full of malice and vengeance?

There is a better reason for having an open mind, and that is your own fallibility. Although there are lots of double-checks built into the investigative procedure to catch you before you report something that isn't true, if you let your emotions guide your activities you'll end up blinded to obvious signs that you're completely on the wrong track. Such emotional blindness has led many investigators into seeing conspiracies where there are none, and wanting to prove their own conspiracy theory, such investigators have published volumes of useless rubbish. I hope the double-checks suggested in the last chapter of this manual prevent you from actually reporting rubbish (a very embarrassing situation), but only your own open mind will save you lost time and energy pursuing a dead-end course that your emotions may be set on following.

That's one lesson I learned the hard way. Several years ago someone convinced me that the Ku Klux Klan was involved in a long-term conspiracy with some domestic Nazi groups and with the John Birch Society. I fell for the bait -- conspiracy theories are somehow very alluring -- and spent quite a while uncovering circumstantial evidence that seemed (to me) to show that a conspiracy existed. Well, in fact, there was no such conspiracy and I wasted about six months work following a stupid lead. Had I kept an open mind and always considered that I could have been wrong about the conspiracy theory, I would have saved myself about six months of research because the evidence against such a conspiracy is overwhelming.

5) Don't become a provocateur. This is a tricky area. It helps to remember that as an investigator you're in search of facts that *already* exist. As long as you're up-front about who you are and what you're doing, you can verbally provoke your subject to blows if you like. That's legitimate although you can well do without the blows. As John or Jane Doe, private citizen, you can try to arrange things so that if the subject is engaged in a pattern and practice of illegal behavior she or he exhibits it to you. For example, it's OK to work with people of a different race to see if a business is discriminating on the basis of race. By applying for a job or trying to rent a house you are not soliciting illegal behavior and you're on solid ground. But if you ask someone, for example, to sell you an illegal drug, you are on very shaky ground because it's usually illegal to buy the drug. That is the kind of entrapment that may send you into court as a defendant or will invalidate any legal case you may have built against your subject. In general it's OK to put yourself into a position of *being* solicited, but don't put yourself into the position of actively soliciting an illegal act.

If an investigation ever requires you to infiltrate an organization, you must never provoke or suggest any action to the organization or to its members. And the warning is "never, never" if you're thinking about something illegal. In that situation you're no longer exposing the crooks, you *are* the crook.

Those are the five basic ethical ground-rules for your investigations. If you stick to them you should be safe. Just about anything outside of those ground-rules goes. Beyond those basics the rest of whatever bag of "professional ethics" you choose to carry around is purely a matter of personal style. As a general guideline, go with the style you're most comfortable with.

Lingering Myths

In case you have any illusions left about what currently passes as "investigative journalism" in the major news media, here is what I hope will be a final blow to the establishmentarian myth: most of the major exposes published by the major media, including the *New York Times* and such electronic media programs as *60 Minutes*, are not original work! Most of the things that appear as "major investigative pieces" in these wealthy media are cannibalized from someone else's Investigations. (Of course, the major media are pretty good about keeping this secret -- they seldom give credit, or even money, to the original investigator.) This is one of the biggest and most shameful rip-offs in the media business today.

For many years the major media got many of their so-called investigative reports from FBI sources as part of the Bureau's

Cointelpro operation. Bureau agents, acting to further the operation "leaked" dozens (maybe hundreds) of stories to favored journalists. Many journalists swallowed the FBI stories hook, line and sinker, some because they were gullible, and others because they wanted to do the Bureau a favor -- also, it didn't hurt these reporters' careers to have a string of major exposes linked to their names. As people who have filed Freedom Of Information Act requests with the Bureau have been able to prove, many of the Bureau's spoon-fed "exposes" were complete fabrications, designed only to discredit certain targets. Had so-called "investigative reporters" of that era been competent, they would have double-checked the FBI handouts and never run many of those defamatory stories.

The FBI, my sources say, is no longer handing out quite so many free "investigative reports" to its cohorts in the media. This cut-off left a lot of journalists and publications with an information crisis of immense proportions. For a while, it must have seemed to some editors and writers that they would actually have to sully their academically honed pencils with some muckraking of their own to fill the gap left by the FBI pull-out.

Fortunately for major publications like the *New York Times* and the *Washington Post*, Congressional committees were still ready to leak convenient stories, but other media were left empty-handed. It was at this point that media attitudes made a sudden flip-flop. During the time FBI handouts were plentiful there was a thriving "underground" or "alternative" press in most major cities. These papers were shunned as outcasts from the media community by the "respectable" media conglomerates still on the FBI handout list. But with the FBI gone from the publishing scene, television networks, wire services, and even the *Times* began to go to the alternative muckraking press for their "investigative" reports. Ironically, and in part because of major media cooperation with the FBI, the alternative press is no longer thriving.

Remnants of the once-thriving alternative and underground press have, however, been the source of "investigative" reports for the major media since about 1976. I know -- I wrote for just such a "disreputable" muckraking tabloid. From six months to a year after one of my investigations was published, it would surface -- virtually word-for-word -- in a "respectable" national publication. Naturally, it had someone else's byline and my muckraking tabloid never got any of the credit for breaking the story. In just two years' of work I developed a file of more than two dozen stories that were cannibalized from mine (not counting the stories that were taken from the first cannibalized version). Other good muckrakers tell much the same story.

Once you understand this cannibalization process, you will know better than to believe anything you see or hear in the major media (despite their claims of objectivity). One example should convince you. A while ago I placed a three paragraph exclusive story in a far-left journal. Less than a week later as I was sitting down for dinner the television newscaster led with *my* story, almost word-for-word. It was perfectly obvious that they hadn't even checked out its accuracy: if they had, they would have come up with at least one sentence that wasn't plagarized. Out of curiosity I called the television station and asked where they got the story. The newscaster said that it had come over a major wire service. (For an interesting semi-monthly running commentary on media atrocities, I suggest a subscription to *AIM Report*, published by Accuracy In Media, Inc., 777 14th St. N.W., Suite 427, Washington, D.C. 20005. Cost is $15 a year.)

In addition to the remnants of the alternative press, another currently favored source of materials for the biggies of the media empire is the local "throwaway" community newspaper. Currently some of the best investigative reporting is to be found in just such "throwaways". Finally, in 1979, the media establishment recognized this and awarded the *Point Reyes Light* a Pulitzer Prize for its reporting on Synanon (long after the major media had cannibalized its work).

Other nationally reported "exposes" that were at least partly cannibalized from "throwaways" that year included a *60 Minutes* feature on George Mitchell WerBell III, a soldier of fortune and arms trader. By now you probably have the message, so it should come as no surprise to you that the "throwaway" stories on WerBell were cannibalized by a Manhattan throwaway as part of a feature on the U.S. Labor Party. Materials from the Manhattan throwaway were later used as part of "exposes" on the U.S. Labor Party by the *New York Times* and *Washington Post*. Naturally, none of the "throwaways" involved got either money or recognition for their work by either the television network or the dailies.

Contemporary muckrakers earning less than subsistence salaries at alternative or throwaway newspapers take heart from the fact that if it wasn't for them the skuldudgery they uncover would be completely suppressed. These men and women are part of a growing club of "public service" journalists spending much of their time and energy preserving what is left of democracy for the rest of us by taking to heart the biblical injunction that "the truth shall set you free".

CHAPTER 2
WHAT TO LOOK FOR

Harry's Fourth Law of investigative reporting: **Go for the jugular.** Let's face it. If you're going to spend your time, money, and a lot of energy trying to get the dirt on someone or some organization, you'll feel much better when you're done if your information causes your subject some serious trouble.

You must, when thinking about your subject, ask yourself what that subject has done (or could have done) that he, she, or it could *really* get in trouble for. It is this kind of analysis that will build the investigative hypothesis you will work to prove.

Take this as a fairly common example of a subject who is an elected official: *a)* he once belonged to the Communist Party (or the Ku Klux Klan); *b)* his son is a homosexual but no one is aware of it and the official opposes gay rights; *c)* he smokes grass and occasionally uses cocaine; *d)* ten years ago he was hospitalized for alcoholism; *e)* he inflates his publicly-funded expense account and pockets the change; *f)* he has had lunch with two known organized crime kingpins; *g)* he takes bribes in exchange for votes on certain legislation.

Now, let's say that you think you can probably prove all of those allegations. The question you must answer is, which allegation are you going to spend your time investigating? None of the charges will help his public image, and depending on what community he represents, some of them would insure that he never ran for office again. But there is only one charge that could put him in jail for a long time -- accepting bribes.

Up until a decade ago, personal "scandals" were enough to dethrone a public figure and cause havoc to private persons. Even in more recent times information from people's private lives has been enough to do them in. Remember Wayne Hayes? Remember Thomas Eagleton? Remember McCarthyism? In some cases personal scandals may still be enough to ruin someone's career. Use them if you have the stomach for it. Personally, I think people's private lives are their own business if they don't intrude into their public lives. If a judge smokes grass at home but comes to court and does a good job, I'd forget about the grass. It's when the judge comes to court stoned, or when he lets his dealer off scot free that the personal becomes public.

Harry's Fifth Law of investigative reporting: **There's nothing like a good felony rap to really cut your subject's jugular.**

Failing a felony rap, certain types of misdemeanors can also get the job done.

By now you have the point: if you're going to be a good investigator you will have to become familiar with what is legal and what isn't. It is good news for the investigator and probably bad news for democracy, but every day hundreds of things that were once legal become crimes. If you don't believe it, take a look at back issues of the *Federal Register*. The *Register* is where the bureaucracy announces its newest policies and interpretations of Congressional Acts. Violations of these policies and interpretations can often mean substantial fines. In 1976 the *Register* contained 21,914 pages of proposed new regulations. By 1978 it had grown to 27,337 pages. And by the end of 1979 it was nearly 35,000 pages! And some of those pages include three or more regulations. Even if you only count the pages, that's about one hundred new regulations a day. And don't forget all the laws that state legislatures, Congress, and local governments are busy passing. Some state legislatures pass as many as 1,000 new criminal laws each year!

Obviously, you'll never know all of the laws -- not even the government knows them all. What you do need is a general sense for the kinds of things that are probably against the law. As you progress with your investigations your work will probably lead you into specialization in one or more areas. But even at that point it's still good to have a general idea of what's legal and illegal in fields other than your own. Don't let this scare you. You do not have to be a lawyer. Reading a few criminal justice texts and similar books should be sufficient. When you need to check whether or not something is actually illegal you can always call the appropriate enforcement agency -- who will often send you a copy of the whole body of laws dealing with your question -- or get a law student or legal librarian to look up the information for you.

It is also a good habit to read reports of court cases in local newspapers. Generally (but not always), these reports will mention the specific charges that the defendant is facing.

The more laws you know, the better your odds of nailing

someone. Think about it.

Your familiarity with the law is what will make you a more effective investigator than the next person.

Here's an example of how knowledge of the law can really help you. A couple of years ago I was interviewing the friend of a subject. The friend knew better than to tell me any of the subject's activities that she knew were illegal. But, as friends often do, especially when they can drop names, the woman did a bit of bragging about her friend and mentioned that in the last month he had received a contract from a South African government official to write some press releases for the American media. The friend didn't know it, but people who take jobs like that have to register with the U.S. Justice Department as agents of a foreign government. The law is the Foreign Agents Registration Act of 1938. Violations carry a stiff penalty, but in peacetime the penalties for this felony are usually ignored. The friend's slip, however, after a check with the Justice Department that turned up the fact that the subject had not registered, was enough to make sure the subject lost a great many of his American clients who were a bit hesitant to give their work to someone who appeared to have enough to hide that he refused to register.

As you become more familiar with various laws, you'll be surprised to learn how many supposedly hostile sources will brag about things that are actually illegal! And your eyes will be opened to the thousands of stories that the mass media miss every day of the year.

So, for final emphasis, *Harry's Sixth Law:* **Know the law.**

# # #

For my purposes I like to classify crimes into two types:
- Violent crimes that physically hurt another person -- like murder, rape, assault
- and, everything else

Lawyers and law enforcement officials of course have their own classifications, but this is not a law course. I use these categories because it makes things easier for me, not because it's necessarily correct.

Violent Crimes

Investigating violent crimes has always been tempting to me, as it is to many other journalists and investigators. Maybe the fascination comes from watching too many detective shows on television. But, more likely, my fascination comes from the fact that it is really challenging to try to prove something that someone else can't prove. And sometimes there is reason to suspect that police overlook some violent crimes because they are pressured into solving the so-called "sexy" crimes. Run-of-the-mill murders, or killings of poor people, for example, sometimes seem to get shoved way down on the police priority list. Then there's another motivation: some of the crimes the police can't solve tend to be the most interesting ones, like a string of murders out in California called the Zodiac killings.

This is all very tempting. But you should be aware that your chances of solving a violent crime that the police cannot solve are about one in a thousand, or worse.

Perhaps even more depressing is that you will develop evidence which to your mind (and almost everyone else's mind) proves your case, only to find that what you consider to be "proof" isn't enough to get your criminal convicted. That's why organizations like the FBI try to nail major crooks on violations of the IRS Code.

For a good example of the kind of investigative work that leads to "proof" of who did the crime but is not enough to do any good in court, I suggest you read *THE TEAMSTERS*, by Steven Brill. It is a superb investigation into the death of Jimmy Hoffa (and an excellent source on corruption in the Teamster union).

I once spent almost a year investigating a series of murders in southern California that had all the experts stumped. We called them the Holiday killings. There were about a dozen murders in a two year period. Each of them happened on a holiday. In each case the victim was a young male who had run away from home. In each case the victim had been raped by one or more men, tortured, chopped into bloody pieces and dumped on a beach. The style of torture indicated that the murderer was the same in each case. My co-researcher and myself had an "in" that the police officials did not. We had contacts in southern California's male homosexual subculture that were fairly extensive and that were inaccessible to the police. So, we thought, we would solve the crime of the decade, write a book about it, get rich, and retire.

Eventually we developed quite a case against two wealthy men who had a special fascination not only with younger men, but with ritualistic "black magic" sadomasochistic activities. What convinced us that we had finally nailed the murderers was a witness who was not killed but was able to describe the suspects' ritual sadomasochism. As it turned out, our suspects used a contraption of ropes and chains that left marks that were identical to those marks found on the bodies of the Holiday murder victims!

By this stage of our investigation we were cooperating with police officials in the three counties where the bodies had been dumped and as we told the officer in charge of the investigation about our witness we were already seeing visions of a very lucrative movie contract from our story.

It was a good circumstantial case. The trouble was, there wasn't a single item of tangible evidence to link our suspects to the bodies.

So far as I know, the case is still open.

But after putting in a year of hard work and coming so close only to have our suspects get off without even spending a night in jail, I resolved never to investigate violent crimes again. As I said, I like to go for the jugular. You can have all the information in the world, but it doesn't do the job unless it can stand up in court.

Had I listened to some advice at the time, I would have saved a lot of time and money. The advice, from a district attorney, was simple: in violent crimes if the suspect isn't caught within the first 48 hours, the chances of ever catching her or him are almost zero.

It's useful to remember, however, that the kind of person who can murder a dozen people usually doesn't have a great deal of respect for other laws. I take some satisfaction from what another investigator-friend told me about a year ago: one of our Holiday murder suspects was eventually sent to prison for insurance fraud.

The lesson from all of that is: if you want to nail someone, it's a lot easier to get them for crimes that aren't violent -- that great classification "other crimes".

Other Crimes

Among the easiest of these "other crimes" to solve fall into what some people classify as "victimless crimes". I call them "street crimes". These include drug-pushing, prostitution, kiddy-porn rings, smuggling, and parole or probation violation. I've done some of this and frankly have found it very boring. It's just too easy. People on the street talk, and it seems that most street-people are pretty familiar with just about everything that's going on in their turf. If those kind of crimes are your thing, that's the key to investigating them: begin by developing friendships with people who know what is going on.

I'll give an example of how easy most "street" crimes are to investigate. A few years ago a good friend of mine swore that a person who was very close to a key member of the White House staff was involved in a subway token racket in New York City. As a favor, I agreed to investigate. I entered New York cold -- without a single contact there. I took a taxi from LaGuardia into town and asked the cab driver what he knew about the subway token racket. Apparently it's something that just about everyone in the Big Apple knows about and the taxi driver sketched out the operation in detail. Like any forgery operation or counterfeit scam, it involved key people who controlled the equipment to produce phony subway tokens. Hundreds of thousands of tokens were produced and then sold to dealers for a nickle apiece. And, like drugs, the more hands the tokens went through, the higher the price and the lower the profit for the dealer. Knowing the pattern of the operation, it was fairly simple to compare it to what we knew about the subject's lifestyle. The subject showed no signs of having a lot of money, and what money the subject had was pretty easily accounted for in legal activities. So, it was obvious that the subject was not part of the higher echelons of the token racket. About all the evidence my friend had on the subject was that the subject had once sold some tokens for a quarter apiece and there was a witness to that. This information put the subject at the lowest end of the racket -- the street dealer. After a couple of days talking with the subject's neighbors no evidence turned up that the subject did this on a regular basis. In fact, what had probably happened was that the subject had received either a bag of phony tokens or stolen tokens and simply dumped the bag. Hardly a major crime. So, the White House was saved from a scandal and the rumors about the subject and the subway token racket were put to rest once and for all.

If you're after bigger fish than the street hustlers (of whatever variety), there are two ways of approaching your subject: from the bottom up, or from the top down. It's not likely that you'll end up nailing the big fish for street crimes, so look into other areas of the law they're probably violating.

But, if you're after big fish, here are two more pointers that may come in handy and both of them begin in prison. As a general rule it's the little guys who end up taking the rap for their bosses. Once in a very rare while -- especially if they feel they've been ripped off and are facing a very long sentence, these little guys will do almost anything to get back at the boss who did them in. They may talk to you, especially if you can somehow assure them that their cover won't be blown. In this situation you have a slight edge over police officials. If a prisoner tells all to the police he knows that eventually he will be expected to testify in court. At that point, his cover will be blown and he knows his lifespan has been shortened by many years. But you, as a private individual, may be able to assure a potential informant that he or she will be safe from ever having to testify. It's been done (but not by me). The second pointer is one that I used successfully once to nail a ring who made a lot of money smuggling illegal aliens into the country and selling them. Again, it's a story of the little fish taking the rap. In this case the little fish wouldn't talk, probably because his sentence was only five years, a lot less with time off for good behavior. But, the man's *wife* was really mad. She was perfectly willing to give me all the names, dates, and addresses I needed on the condition that I not use her name. Contrary to the stereotype of the mobster's wife who doesn't know anything about her husband's line of work, many wives (and other relatives) *do* know. Often it's a lot easier to get them to talk than it is to get the guy who's doing the time to talk.

Of all of these "street" crimes, the ones that I have found to be most useful are parole and probation violation. The restrictions found in most parole and probation agreements (which the prosecuting attorney will usually be glad to send you a copy of) are generally so absurd that it is almost impossible *not* to violate them.

This is one "street" crime I always store in the back of my mind because it can come in handy in investigations that are totally unrelated to parole or probation. It's another way to go for the jugular. It's easy. And sometimes you get lucky as I did once when I was investigating the leader of one of the several Ku Klux Klan organizations. Some people had urged me to do the investigation because they believed the man was ripping off money from Klan members. There were plenty of witnesses to support that charge, but the man's operation was perfectly legal, so while my contacts had a legitimate gripe, there wasn't much they could do about it. Their Klansman, however, was on parole. One of the terms of his parole was that he not leave the state. As it turned out, one of my sources had seen the subject in another state in violation of his parole. That information, when delivered to the proper authorities, was enough to put the subject out of business for awhile.

Most investigations undertaken by citizen investigators don't deal with either violent or "street" crimes at all. Actually, law enforcement officials generally do a good job of investigating violent crimes -- and, they have the resources to do the job. Investigating "street" crimes, unless it leads to someone in a very public and powerful position (the White House, for example) is generally too boring for the good citizen investigator -- although, if you neighborhood happens to be a hangout for drug pushers and you don't like to have them hanging around, go ahead and investigate. But if you're serious about getting them out of your neighborhood, the best way to do it is to organize your neighbors to patrol the area and call the police when something is coming down. If your protest gets enough media attention the local government may even be forced into beefing up the patrols in your area -- the best deterrent there is.

Most citizen investigations focus on what some people like to call "white collar" crimes. White collar crooks rip off much more money than all the street crooks put together. Not only that, but street hustlers usually operate by mutual consent with their clients. White collar crooks specialize in ripping off people without their "consent". It's one of the greatest rackets going and almost every one of us suffers from them in one way or another.

Conversely, most of us also perpetrate "white collar" crimes --

ever rip off some pencils from your office?

The most exciting thing about "white collar" crime, for me at least, is that it is entirely possible to nail really big fish, people in positions of public trust who use their position to fill their own pockets at our expense. A successful investigation of this kind is not only a big public service, but is personally very gratifying. Much of the rest of this manual is devoted to these kinds of investigations. Most of the techniques discussed, however, apply to all investigations.

White Collar Crimes

The keys to white collar crime investigations are: Motive, Opportunity, and Cover.

Motive is usually pretty obvious in white collar crimes: making money.

Opportunity can be separated into five areas: *1)* any time money changes hands; *2)* any time commodities (including information) changes hands; *3)* any time someone has power that can be used by someone to make a profit; *4)* any time someone has power that can save someone money; *5)* any time someone has power that can be used to spare someone else trouble (like delays in permits, traffic tickets, prison sentences, etc.). As you can see, a whole lot of people have one or another of these opportunities -- including the investigator.

Cover is essential because the crook does not want to get caught. It is here that an investigation usually succeeds in nailing the subject.

If you begin to put together the three elements -- Motive, Opportunity, and Cover -- you'll be able to see a world of potential white collar crimes. I strongly recommend that every investigator use her or his imagination this way because whatever combination you come up with, there is probably a law against it and that's the most effective way to go for the jugular.

So here's *Harry's Seventh Law:* **Think like a crook.** It's good training.

You can put this into practice anywhere just by asking yourself some very cynical questions.

Here are some examples:
- *Someone gets caught stealing dynamite. The court sentence is probation. Question: is there a*

payoff? Of course there is. In this particular case the judge let the man off because he was an FBI informant. MOTIVE: judge wants to advance his career (money). OPPORTUNITY: judge has power to sentence. COVER: a few years down the road the judge will be appointed to a higher bench (he was).

• Someone offers you ten pounds of hamburger for 50¢ a pound. Question: where did he or she steal it? MOTIVE: your money. OPPORTUNITY: her brother works at a meat-packing plant. COVER: the transaction is through a third party and is in cash so there's no record.

• Your neighborhood was zoned residential until a big company wanted to build next door to you. Question: who was paid off? MOTIVE: money. OPPORTUNITY: the city council votes on zoning regulations. COVER: those who voted for the zoning switch got stock in the company.

• Your property tax goes up. A prominent city official hasn't had a tax hike in years. Question: who was paid off? MOTIVE: the tax assessor's cousin wants a government job (money). OPPORTUNITY: the tax assessor determines the value of the property. COVER: the assessor's cousin gets the job.

• All of the new apprentices in your union are coming from one training program even though there are three good programs in the area. Question: Who's getting paid off? MOTIVE: the boss of the training program gets several relatives hired for easy union jobs (money). OPPORTUNITY: key union officials can fix who gets taken on as an apprentice. COVER: the relatives are hired, then give the union official 10% of their pay.

• Every time you write a check and there's no money in your account to cover it, it bounces. But your boss's checks never bounce no matter how far overdrawn he is. Question: who's getting paid off? MOTIVE: the banker wants your boss's business, especially the loans (money). OPPORTUNITY: the *bank manager flags the account so checks are cleared.* COVER: *the banker gets the loans and if he's audited says the rubber checks were covered by a letter of credit.*

All of the examples are not only true, they are very common. And, they are all *very* illegal. Train yourself to notice things that don't follow the normal pattern; to see suspicious circumstances; to be aware of potential conflicts of interest; and then put *Motive, Opportunity,* and *Cover* together into one hypothesis, and you'll probably be on the trail of an exciting investigation!

CHAPTER 3
DO YOUR HOMEWORK

By this chapter, unless you already knew who you wanted to investigate before you began this manual, you will have found some tantalizing subject for your investigation. It doesn't matter if you subject lives in your general area or several states away from you, most of your work can still be done from where you live.

In this chapter we'll look at some of the critical preliminaries to an investigation that a surprising number of people forget. I call it "doing your homework". The purpose of homework is to know the general framework in which your subject functions -- in other words, your subject's environment.

Like much homework, this part of an investigation may seem like a chore you might want to avoid, but it is critical to the rest of your work.

As a result of researching your subject's "environment" you'll develop information that will help you to:
- know what kinds of dirt to look for
- develop a sense of what is irregular and therefore suspicious about your subject's activities
- develop sources for future leads
- know enough to be able to talk to the sources you develop without blowing your investigation
- get a sense of what to expect from your subject and therefore be able to avoid phony leads
- avoid conclusions that are wrong.

Generally, you will have one of two kinds of subjects: an *individual*, or an *organization*. In either case your homework chores will be somewhat similar since both individuals and organizations function within very specific environments. And, of course, these environments overlap. In any case, to simplify things, we'll look at the two types of subjects separately.

Individual

If your subject is an individual -- a living, breathing person and not a corporation -- there are a variety of facts you should develop about your subject in the homework stage. You can begin with basic biographical information. In my own work, I like to develop a kind of chronological history of the subject. Sometimes there are blank spaces that I am too lazy to fill in during the homework stage, and a lot of times I can fill in the spaces as I pursue my investigation.

Before I give you a sample of one of my chronologies, I'll summarize the kinds of information you should try to have:

1) When and where was the subject born?
2) Where, and for how long, did the subject attend school (or say he/she attended school)?
3) What jobs has the subject had, including military service?
4) Where were these jobs, and during what years?
5) What special training has the subject had?
6) What career(s) has the subject had and where?
7) Who are the subject's relatives and where are they now?
8) Where does the subject live now, and in the past?
9) With whom does the subject live now, and in the past?
10) Has the subject had children? Where are they now?
11) Has the subject been divorced? Where is/are former spouse(s)?
12) If the subject is active in a religion or cult, what is it and what does he/she do there?
13) If the subject is active in organizations, what are they and what does he/she do in them?
14) What religious or organizational ties did the subject have in the past?
15) What is the subject's financial position?
16) Where did the subject get his/her money? Property?
17) Is the subject active in politics? If so, in what groups and doing what? What are the subject's political views? What is the subject's past political history?
18) Does the subject have a criminal history? What is it?
19) Does the subject have any health problems? What are they?
20) Does the subject drink? How much?
21) Is the subject involved in socially disapproved or illegal activities in his/her personal life: e.g., uses dope, is gay, etc.
22) Are any of the subject's relatives dependent on him/her for financial assistance? Why, and how much assistance?
23) What are the subject's hobbies and favorite leisure activities?
24) Has the subject ever used a different name? What was it?
25) Would the subject's job require a security clearance?

You can probably add lots of things to this list. Now let's look at how this information can be useful to you.

Many of the details are primarily useful as sources of more information: items 1, 2, 4, 6, 7, 8, 9, 10, 11, 12, 13, 14, 17, and 23. Information about relatives, schools, places the subject has lived, organizations, religious activities, and professional associations can all be leads to where you can look for more information. You may want to check out the subject's family standing -- a good place to begin is where he/she was born and who his/her parents were. Schools have yearbooks that include lots of information (you may also discover that the subject is lying about graduating from a specific school). Organizations provide contacts who may know the subject, as do religious groups. A subject's business associates may not be eager to talk, but they're good to know about and there are ways to get them to talk.

Putting many of the items together will give you some insight into the subject's personality: Does he/she keep jobs or lose them? Move a lot? "Love them and leave them"?

Drinking and/or other habits may give you an insight into how to approach the subject when the time comes. It may seem like a television trick, but in fact, many things have been learned by getting a subject drunk enough to tell all. Things like using dope and being gay let you know that your subject makes contact with very specific subcultures -- places where you may find people willing to talk about the subject.

Some aspects of the subject's business or private life may require that he/she be licensed or have earned special degrees. You may find that your subject isn't licensed after all. Nearly ten years ago, for example, I went for some help to a person who advertised on his business card that he was a clinical psychologist. He began to overcharge me and get very nasty about wanting money I couldn't give him. A quick call to the state licensing agency turned up the fact that he wasn't licensed to practice clinical psychology. After I told him what I'd found, he never sent any more bills. As he was fairly active in local politics I could have caused him some mighty big trouble, but I didn't want to. (It's one of the things I've filed for possible future reference.)

Other aspects of the subject's life history may make you

suspicious. One state senator I investigated, for example, started out without owning anything and had no wealthy relatives. After about ten years in office, he owned a great deal of property -- much more than his salary could account for. It made a great story and the Internal Revenue Service took it from there.

Some of the items you will research as part of your homework may indicate that the subject is under pressure to get money to support some expensive hobby, or perhaps a relative.

Perhaps most important, knowledge of what the subject is doing in his or her life will enable you to develop a feel for what opportunities he/she has to get money illegally *and* what set of laws regulate the subject's life. A printer, for example, has the opportunity to print bogus money and other documents. A pharmacist has access to drugs. A banker has access to money and information. A politician has access to power. A lobbyist has the opportunity to bribe someone.

Anyone who owns a business is plagued by laws: labor codes, Occupational Safety and Health regulations, National Labor Relations Board regulations, and laws specific to certain industries. Officers and directors of corporations that trade stock are bound by a variety of Securities and Exchange Commission laws. Bankers are regulated, stock brokers are regulated, bakers are regulated, and so on and on.

The next phase of your homework, then, is to learn what set of laws affect your subject's business activities and to familiarize yourself with these laws so that you will be able to know when they are being violated. This may be the most difficult part of your homework. But there's one consolation -- after you learn about a certain set of laws you generally don't have to go through it again. Most businesses, trades and professions are regulated by one or more federal agencies and one or more state agencies. In the appendix of this manual you will find a good reference to a source that lists most federal regulatory agencies. A couple of phone calls should fill your mailbox with hundreds of pages of regulations that apply to your subject. Or, you can call the Federal Information Center. It describes its purpose as "a small office that is equipped to answer specific questions about government agencies and will direct the caller to the particular agency which could best answer his/her questions. It is a referral service to the federal government".

Simply call them (816-374-2466) and ask them to refer you to the appropriate government agency. If you prefer writing, the address is: 601 E. 12th St., Kansas City, MO 64106. With state agencies, you are on your own. Generally a telephone directory of the state capital will have a listing of state agency headquarters. Try the agency that you *think* is relevant. If you've got the wrong agency, someone there might be able to refer you to another agency.

Another way to pick up on laws that are pertinent to a trade or profession is to read the trade publication that is published for members. (Some are better than others.) There are a couple of references in the appendix that should help you here. Reading the "trades", as they are called, is also a good way to learn important details of your subject's professional subculture. You'll be using this information later when you talk to your sources and want to sound like you know what you're talking about. The "trades" will also give you some ideas about what kinds of questions you will want to ask.

Now for the third part of your homework. The profile you've drawn of your subject should provide you with enough information for you to be able to fit into your subject's environment. If he or she is a banker, for example, you will want to know how banks operate, what bankers actually do, etc. an important aspect of this research phase is to pick up any of the special slang that is used in your subject's environment.

You will also want to know "who's who" in your subject's environments: in his/her professional life, religion, and any organizations he/she might belong to. The purpose of this is, as with the slang, so that when you're talking to possible sources you will "fit in" better. Sources are much less likely to be suspicious of you if you understand what they're talking about and can keep up a good conversation.

So, you will want to do at least a mini-profile of some of the key organizations your subject belongs to Before getting to that, however, look at one of my sample profiles (I call them chronologies) for an idea of what your initial homework should give you. You'll note that I don't have all of the questions answered. You'll also note that I make a pretty clear distinction between what I know is fact and what someone has told me or what is rumor.

Chronology: Lyndon Hermyle LaRouche, Jr. aka Lyn Marcus

1922	Sept. 10, born, Rochester NH, parents Quakers, family history allegedly goes back to colonial period
	father, allegedly management consultant for shoe manufacturer (one hostile source says father owned co.)
	both parents now dead
	sisters, 2 younger, location unknown
	myopic since childhood
	early address, 3 Coxeter Square
	grammar school, School St. School, Rochester
	parents had summer home in Strafford, NH
	in youth, family active as Quakers
	few friendships in school, high school "friends" at chess games
1939	began working during summers
????	becomes conscientious objector, says because of father
	joins Army
1944	leaves for Burma, then serves in India. some reports say as medical corpsman, others say he was in OSS
1947	attends Northeastern University, MA
1948	drops out of university, says takes "consulting" job
	joins Socialist Workers Party
	toured with SWP candidate Grace Carlson
	Donald Morrill, an army acquaintance introduced him to SWP (wife Sue)
	LaRouche apparently in Lynn, MA at this time
	Stanley Lippman (wife Mary) also friend
	Benjamin Fishman also friend
1950-52	an undefined job travelling through Mississippi Valley & Southwest
1954?	took consulting job in NYC, wanted to be near center SWP action
1954-55?	gets married, reportedly has one son, wife said to be psychiatrist
1959	begins computer firm
1960	final break with SWP, divorce from wife(?)
1963	severs relationship with above-mentioned computer applications co.

41

1963?	reportedly begins living with Carol Schnitzer reportedly tried to organize own leftist groups with Schnitzer
1966	began giving classes at Greenwich Village Free U. under name "Lynn Marcus". Schnitzer also reportedly gave classes students from classes to become cadre of new group
1968	he and Carol apparently took control of Students for Democratic Society Labor Committee in NYC. squabble over strike at Columbia U. he was apparently kicked out of SDS, but took some labor committees with him. this was to become the core of his new National Caucus of Labor Committees
1969	travels to Canada, organization begins publishing *Solidarity,* sued by AFL-CIO & changes name to *New Solidarity*
1970	FBI opens file on group, will total 5,000 pp. FBI said had two informers in NCLC
1972	Carol Schnitzer apparently leaves LaRouche trip to Germany(?)
1973	returns from Europe, reportedly consolidates all NCLC power in self
????	Carol Schnitzer apparently marries British NCLC member, Christopher White
1973-74	LaRouche alleges White programmed to assassinate him, "de-programming session begins". Note: Carol & Christopher apparently still married and active in NCLC in 1980
1973-	SEE ORGANIZATION PROFILE

...1976, runs for president...1980, runs for president...

The profile of the two-time presidential candidate continues in a similar vein and is continually updated as new information is added. Every couple of months, especially in an active investigation, it is a good idea to rewrite the chronology so that you have at your fingertips a simple and complete summary.

From this short chronology, you can see that there are already several possible leads that could be followed. School chums in New Hampshire may remember him; professors at Northeastern University may have some interesting material on his friends and activities; some friends have been named who, if located, could provide even more background. Notice also that there is probably a divorce record in 1960 and a former wife who might be located and may be willing to talk. Notice also the record in 1969 of an AFL-CIO suit against *Solidarity.* This suggests that this union probably has substantial files on the case and probably on LaRouche himself.

Chronologies like these help me in three ways. First, the more often I look at them, the more ideas I get for future leads. Second, it is an easy way to put events and people into a time frame -- often, *when* someone does something can be important in understanding both motive and opportunity.

In addition to the chronology on a primary investigative subject you should also develop the following: a set of index cards with the names of each person you have found who has been associated with your subject; and profiles of the organizations your subject has been involved in. As your investigation progresses, you will develop more and more leads to people who know or knew your subject, and you'll fill in the details you can get about these contacts -- their current address, phone number, etc. In some cases these index-carded contacts will be important enough to your investigation to warrant chronologies of their own.

Many investigators try to get a photo of their subject and any contacts, as well as descriptive information. This is useful when you need to ask someone if they can identify your subject. It also tests your contact's credibility -- if your source claims to know the subject very well and you show the source a packet of ten photos and the source can't pick out the photo of your subject, then you know you've been had.

Sources for Chronologies

If your subject is active in public life (involved in politics, a leader in his or her profession, a community organizer, an officer of some organization, or any other kind of "celebrity", your task of building a chronology is greatly simplified. The first two sources you'll go to are in any large public library: various *WHO'S WHO* books, and newspaper files.

There is a *WHO'S WHO* of virtually every group you can think of: doctors, psychologists, writers, politicians, business leaders, eductaors, etc. There are, in many areas of the country, even local *WHO'S WHO* books. Some of the "who's who" type directories go under different titles, so ask your librarian for help locating the books that are most likely to mention your subject. Also, be sure to try to go through as many back editions as possible -- entries change from year to year. Your subject may not be listed one year, but you may find listings from five or even ten years ago. The information you'll find is usually provided by the subject and is often sketchy. But it's a good start. A typical listing will include date of birth, place of birth, eduction, career data, and major achievements.

The second major source your library offers are its newspaper files. Usually libraries have both local papers and, on microfilm, back files of the *Washington Post,* the *New York Times,* and the most prominent newspaper in your general region. The *New York Times* and a few other papers are indexed. Call around to your local libraries before visiting them to make sure that they have the papers *and* the indexes.

If your subject happens to appear by name in the index, you've found a bonanza without much time or trouble. Just look up the articles, get copies of them, and stick them in your file for future reference.

If your subject isn't indexed then you should see if there are references to his or her organizations. Look at these articles. If they seem to be helpful, keep them.

If neither your subject nor the organizations are indexed you have just run into a wall that it will take some time and creativity to either tunnel under or jump over.

There are two approaches at this point. If you know enough about your subject to know approximately what year(s) he or she may have made news, then you can consider going through the local or regional papers during that time one page at a time. Or, you can call the editor of your local paper or the biggest regional paper and ask if he or she remembers when (or if) the paper did an article on your subject or organization. Sometimes you'll be lucky and be turned over to a reporter who has covered your subject.

When Luck Runs Out

If your subject is turning to be an apparent nonentity, don't give up hope -- any tiny bit of information you can get on your subject for your chronology during the homework stage will be important later. Search your memory for anything you may

already know about your subject besides his or her name. Here is a list of questions that may be helpful:
- *What city or state does your subject live in?*
- *About how old is your subject?*
- *Where do you think your subject was born?*
- *What groups do you think your subject is active in?*
- *Where do you think your subject works?*

Once you have asked yourself these questions, here is what to do with the information:

- *If you have a city or state, look up your subject in the phone directory of the city or of the largest cities in the state... maybe even the smallest towns. This may at least give you an address and phone number. Also, don't forget to look at old directories. Some subjects may have decided they don't want to be listed now, but they may have been listed a few years ago.*
- *If you know about how old your subject is, you can probably figure out when he or she went to school. Combine this information with information you have about the subject's location and then look through school libraries and locate your subject in one or more of their yearbooks or school newspapers.*
- *If you know where your subject was born, you can look up early information from phone books and school yearbooks.*
- *If you know what groups your subject is active in, then call them saying you are an old friend and see if anyone in these organizations knows where your subject is now and what he or she is doing today.*
- *If you know where your subject works, there are two possible approaches: 1) ask people who work at the company about your subject -- say you think you may have known the subject in grade school or something, 2) pretend you are a personnel officer of another company and are verifying the subject's references with the company's personnel officer; or, you might pretend you are checking your subject's application for a loan or credit card.*

If your subject served in the military, there is a chance the local veterans' group may know him or her.

If you can find your subject's car and get its license plate you should be able to get a current address from the state department of motor vehicles.

These are by no means all of the leads you should follow if you're running into a dead end. I can think of at least a dozen more. But by now you have the general idea. Your best resource is yourself: you are the one who can come up with new ideas in search of information about your subject. Also, the books listed in the resource section should inspire your creativity!

Organization Profiles

In many ways organization profiles are much easier to do than profiles on individual people. The reasons for this are threefold. First, most organizations have filed one or another document with some arm of the government and these documents are available to the public. They provide a lot of great information. Second, organizations tend to have members. This means that there is a pool of people who have information about the organization they may be willing to share. Third, most organizations *try* to do something, and so records about them may turn up in newspapers or other public documents.

One of the techniques I've found most successful in beginning to profile an organization is to obtain copies of whatever literature they may produce. Usually, this involves sending the group some money for a subscription to their newsletter, or sending a contribution to one of their efforts (in return for which you will receive literature asking you to send more money). If the group is one that you think may be dangerous, then get your information under an assumed name and at a post office box.

From this literature you should get a variety of information: the legal status of the group (is it a non-profit group, a political action committee, a business, etc.?); names of leaders of the group as well as important members; addresses and phone numbers. One caution here: save everything you are sent, including the envelopes, and make sure you note the date that you received the information.

Most organizations that are serious about what they are trying to accomplish will incorporate. This theoretically will protect the individual officers of the corporation from being sued if the group itself gets into trouble, and, it simply sounds more impressive to new recruits and members to be able to say the group is incorporated. It is also wonderful for the investigator because the group's articles of incorporation are public record, as are any amendments to them. Additionally, some states require that some corporations file annual reports that are also a matter of public record.

Your first step in tracing a corporation is to determine what state the group incorported in. Most often it will be the state that their main office is located in. However, for a variety of reasons, the group may be incorporated in some other state. At this point your research is simply a matter of calling the Secretary of State's office to check if your subject corporation exists in their files. If it does, you can, for a small fee, purchase copies of the articles of incorporation, the by-laws, amendments, and annual reports. Some states require that corporations give more information than others, but whatever you can get will help you.

If you try the state where the corporation appears to have its main office and there is no record of the corporation, then you'll have to search. Attorneys who specialize in this can charge up to $500, sometimes more, for this search, but you can do it easily and cheaply from your own phone. Here are some hints that might speed up your search if the corporation isn't where you think it should be: 1) most corporations incorporate in Delaware, so try that state first; 2) organizations that operate out of Washington, D.C. often incorporate in Virginia, so try that state next -- if they're not in Virginia, then try Maryland; 3) as the next step, try the states nearest to the state you think they belong in; 4) if none of these maneuvers have worked, then try New York, California, Missouri, and Illinois. If none of these have located your corporation, then continue checking every other state, starting with those that it is the least expensive for you to call.

Your last states will probably be Alaska and Hawaii -- you may prefer to write rather than to call.

If you have finished with all 50 states and can find no record of your corporation, then you have possibly caught the group violating one state law or another. It is against the law for a corporation to do business in a state unless it has registered there. And "doing business" includes such simple things as mailing out newsletters. At this point, if you like, you can go to your state attorney with your phone call records and see if he or she will begin an investigation. If you get an investigation, the attorney you work with will probably be pretty happy to share information with you.

# # # #

If your subject organization claims to be a tax-deductible non-profit group, you are on the verge of uncovering dozens of pages of information about your subject. It is much simpler, and requires less disclosure of information, for an organization to incorporate than it is for it to gain the benefits of federal non-profit status. So, if your subject is non-profit, call an Internal Revenue Service press officer (202-566-4021) who will be more than happy to provide you with information about the laws regulating non-profit organizations, and will tell you who to talk to for a search of IRS records for filings made by your organization. Be sure to get a copy of your organization's application for exemption (it will include the articles of incorporation and bylaws filed with the state), as well as all available copies of the group's annual reports. Depending on the type of exemption, different report forms are required. Usually, annual reports are only available for the past five or so years, but they are still worthwhile.

With this package from the IRS, for which you'll pay a small fee to cover copying, you will find a great deal of information about your subject. You'll find what the group has told the government it does (if it's doing something else, it may lose its exemption), its sources of money, its total annual budget, what non-money assets it owns, and how it spends its money. Also you will find the names, and occasionally other information, about the organization's directors and officers. Once in a while, you'll even find social security numbers of some directors -- this can help you if you ever want to check the background of the directors.

Unfortunately for the investigator, not all tax-exempt groups are required to make such extensive filings for the public. Beyond articles of incorporation, for example, you won't find anything at all on churches -- which is why they are often good shelters for other non-religious activities.

Before a group can get a federal exemption, it must have already received an exemption form the state. Records of these transactions are available to you from the Secretary of State. Individual states, however, seldom require much information from a group before granting an exemption, so you may be disappointed by what you find there.

If your subject is a union or "labor organization" you are also in luck. Each union (and each local of the larger unions) is required not only to make certain filings with the IRS that are open to public inspection, but must file an annual report with the Department of Labor. This report will provide the investigator with many interesting gems of information. Basically, the report is designed to show how the union spent its money. Usually the most interesting part of these reports is the section that lists the salaries and expenses of union employees. In some union reports you will notice that many salaried officials have the same last names -- they are often relatives. Whenever you see relatives hiring each other, be alert -- corruption often follows. You may also notice that expenses listed for employees seem a bit high -- another area you should be suspicious of. It is also sometimes worthwhile, if the union you are researching is a local of a larger union, to look into the group's parent. You may find that some of the employees of your local are also getting paid by the parent union. The specific report you are looking for is "Labor Organization Annual Report, Form LM-2". The Department of Labor is a fairly complex bureaucracy to work through. You should definitely get help from the DOL's office of public information at 202-523-7316 when you begin to search for union reports. Again, be prepared to pay a small fee.

If your organization is a political group that supports one or more candidates for federal office (or if your subject is a candidate), you are if for a public records bonanza. Each of these groups that spend more than $500 are required by law to file regular reports with the Federal Elections Commission. (Some may also have to file copies of their reports with your Secretary of State.) The Federal Elections Commission (FEC) was, as of 1980 at least, a public investigator's dream come true -- and a nightmare for candidates themselves. FEC reports are computerized and can be purchased by mail. The phone call is even free: 800-424-9530. When you first ask for campaign reports made by your group, the FEC will mail you a computer-printout summary of what it has available and how much you will have to pay for copying. These summaries are free and occasionally can supply valuable information on their own, most often how much money the candidate or committee has already received in contributions. When ordering copies of FEC reports be sure to get the "Statement of Organization" and any correspondence between the FEC and the group. If you're lucky either the statement of organization or the correspondence will include material on the group's (or their attorney's) letterhead which will give you a list of organization leaders you might not otherwise have.

The FEC requires that groups report the name, address, and occupation of every person who has contributed $100 or more to the campaign. Sometimes this information can be valuable and it is usually worth your money to at least have a look at this section of the organization's report. The FEC also requires that the group report all of its expenditures. This section of the report will tell you what companies the group is dealing with, who is on its staff, who it pays as consultants, etc.

The only problem with FEC reports is that when you are researching a very active organization, their reports may run into thousands of pages and that can cost you a lot of money. You have three choices: *1)* hire a competent researcher in the District of Columbia who can look through the reports and copy only the information you want; *2)* buy everything; or *3)* try to select specific reports from the list that is available. If you chose the third alternative, you should probably spend your money on the group's first reports and those reports that it files immediately before and immediately after an election. The first reports will show you who is really behind the group. The election-period reports are generally when the most money changes hands the fastest and is, in my experience, the best bet for finding any illegal transfers of money.

Another hint: if, in any reports from any group you are studying, you find that payments are often made to one or two vendors, it's probably worthwhile to get information about these vendors. Most often they will be incorporated, so go for articles of incorporation. You may find that your group is taking money from the public or from its members in order to enrich the pockets of a company that happens to be owned by one of your group's leaders. With tax-exempt groups this is usually illegal. With unions and political groups it may not be illegal, but it is very suspicious and worth following up.

This list of examples by no means exhausts the public reports that are available to you from the federal government. For example, anyone who has a second-class mailing permit must file annual reports as well as an application for that permit. If someone is using a bulk mail permit you can, by getting a copy of the application for the permit, find out who owns or operates the group using the permit.

Here's another hint about the post office: if your group uses a post office address you can, posing as a citizen who has received an *unsolicited* mailing from that post office box, get the postmaster to tell you in whose name the box is registered. This is one you can even do over the phone.

Lobbying reports can also be gems, even though laws requiring lobbyists to register are not very well enforced and are full of loopholes. Rather than go to the trouble of a telephone attempt to get lobbying information from federal agencies, your best bet is to go to a library that subscribes to *Congressional Quarterly*, a weekly magazine that summarizes who has registered as a lobbyist for whom. Of course, if you find a lobbyist you are interested in, then to get the full report that tells how much money the lobbyist supposedly spent, you'll have to try the government directly. This can be very difficult if you don't live near the District of Columbia. Lobbying reports filed with the U.S. Senate, for example, are not copied for journalists. (In a pinch, your own congressman may be willing to get the information for you if you don't want to hire a researcher in the capitol.) It also generally takes an in-person visit to get lobbying reports filed with the U.S. House of Representatives, but at least you can get copies made of them. Names of lobbyists who file with the House of Representatives can also be found in the *Congressional Record*, but the lazy person is much better off looking through *Congressional Quarterly*.

In general, any time any group gets a license, permit, or tax break from the government -- or any time it is regulated by an agency of the government -- it will have to file a public report somewhere. Only your imagination and ingenuity limits the data you can get on your subject from the government.

If the federal government can be considered an investigator's dream, the opposite is true of state and local governments. State and local filing systems are generally not computerized and require hand searches. Not all civil servants are willing to undertake these searches for you, so getting out-of-state records is sometimes a problem. Generally, however, if you tell the state civil servant that you are a reporter and use some flattery, you will get the help you need. As a general rule, if the federal government has an agency like the Federal Elections Commission or the IRS, your state government will have a similar agency.

Unless you, or your researcher, are in a local community to do searches yourself, don't expect to get much information from local governments. Depending on whose version of the story you wish to believe, local civil servants are either extremely lazy, or are too overworked to deal with telephone or written requests for information. Despite the fact that getting information on file with county or city governments is tedious, if you have the energy for the work they also are potential gold mines. The most useful information you'll probably ever use that's on file in local or county clerks' offices are records of property ownership, records of wills that have gone into probate, birth and death certificates, records of marriages and divorces, and something that's known in the trade as a "dba". A "dba" is a statement that most businesses must file with their county clerks (and publish in local newspapers) that says who owns the business. For example, if Joe Smith starts up a business called Acme Axe Associates, he will have to file a notice that he, Joe Smith, is "doing business as" ("dba") Acme Axe Associates. Such filings will also list any partners he has, his home address, and other potentially useful information.

Organization Summary

The sources of information above may be confusing until you get used to them. Also, you should remember that they are by no means *all* of the sources of public information you can access. As part of your homework stage of investigation you should get copies of every available public record you can about the organization you're researching. Also remember to get on the group's mailing list.

When you're done with all of this "homework" you'll have several thick folders full of documents about your organization. From these you should extract the information to do an organization profile similar to the sample individual profile that appeared a few pages back. In this profile would go the name or names the organization has used, all phone numbers and addresses it has used, all of its subsidiary groups, and, more important, all of the names of people who have had a major role in the organization as officers, salaried employees, or as vendors to it. It's also useful, to accompany the organization profile, if you keep a set of index cards on all of the people associated with the group, filling in the data on these people as you run across it.

Harry's Eighth Law: **Get all of the public records you can.**

(This law has two corollaries: *1)* if your subject is supposed to file something with the government and hasn't done so, the subject has violated the law; and *2)* if your subject has filed information that is false, the subject has probably violated the law.)

To help inspire you as you do the sometimes tedious job of "homework", here's a hint -- during the homework process itself you may find the information you're looking for about your subject and not have to go further. If you follow Harry's Sixth Law, you will find that more and more of your investigations are actually concluded during this homework stage. If that isn't inspiration enough to get you to do your homework, here's *Harry's Ninth Law:* **The more you learn about your subject, the easier it is to learn more.**

CHAPTER 4
DEVELOPING "INSIDE" SOURCES

To those on the outside of the investigative world, the famous "inside sources" investigators develop are a mystery. Actually, the world is a lot smaller than you think, and the source you need to help your investigation is often as close as one or two phone calls away.

The results of one sociologist's experiment should help to convince you of this. Sociologist Stanley Milgram used a computer to select a random sample of Americans. He divided the sample into two groups. One group were "targets", comparable to the subject of an investigation. The second group were in the position of investigators -- it was their job to find someone who knew the "target" personally by using their friends. The odds, according to Milgram, that any one of the investigators would know his or her "target" were 1 in 200,000. The would-be investigators were mailed the name of a "target". If they did not know the "target" personally, they were to forward the name of the "target" to one of their friends. This forwarding process was to continue until the "investigator", by means of this friendship chain, had found someone who knew the "target" personally. You might imagine that the process of connecting the investigator to the target may have taken dozens of intermediaries. Actually, the largest number of intermediaries was 10! The smallest number was 2, and the average number was 5.

What this means is that through your *own* friendship circle you are probably only five people away from the subject of your investigation, no matter where he or she lives in the United States.

That is the first secret of "inside" sources: use your friendship network.

Milgram's study also revealed another important facet of the investigator's knack for developing "inside" sources. During the course of his study of friendship chains described above, he found that often there was one key person who knew most of the "targets". As a description of the study says, "Often there was a 'sociometric star', through whom the target person received most of his envelopes. Whether or not the target person realized it, the sociometric star was a vital link between him and the rest of the world."

That is the second secret of "inside" sources: include in your friendship network key people who know everything and everyone -- "sociometric stars".

Often, you will be surprised at just who some of your friends and acquaintances *do* know. As an example, I recently finished an investigation of the networks that smuggle foreign nationals into the United States illegally to work for slave wages. I knew I wanted to make contact with two groups: smugglers and the people who "bought" the undocumented immigrants. For a person who lives a relatively quiet, middle-class existence, this possibility seemed very remote. But I did what I always do, I talked about my investigation to my friends. As it turned out, one of my friends had a brother who "bought" undocumented immigrants. Another friend had a lover who had previously lived with a smuggler. Because I had developed these "inside" sources through my extended friendship network, both of them trusted me enough to talk to me about their experiences. They also were able to give me even more leads. That's not the first time my friendship network has come in handy, but it is the most intriguing example from my own experience.

Unfortunately, this is a pool of sources that most novice investigators *never* tap. So here is *Harry's Tenth Law:* **Get your friends to help you.**

Not only should you put your friends to work for you, but you should try your neighbors, people you work with, people in your club or organization, and people at the local bar. Between all of these you will probably be able to develop all the "inside" sources you'll ever need. One such source I developed this way held a cabinet position in the White House for two years!

If you want to make your friendship network an even more effective tool, then make friends with a wide variety of people. The purpose of this, of course, is so that you have access to various subcultures that don't usually overlap. For example, if all your friends happen to be black, it's not likely you're going to find an "inside" source in the Ku Klux Klan. However, if you have friends and acquaintances in each group, so much the better for you.

One thing that you should remember in connection with using

your friendship network is to use it with care. Treat your friends as friends. It's only fair. Not only that, but it's the only way to keep your networks in operation. And, you should be prepared to return the favors you ask. Not only that, you shouldn't continually badger the inside sources you do develop. Save them for an emergency. Although I had a good source in the White House, for example, I never used this person. The White House source was my "ace in the hole". It is not only a good way to play poker, it is a good way to stay functioning as an investigator.

Traditional Sources

Your friendship network alone should be enough to keep you well-stocked with all of the sources you will ever need. But it is often better to find other ways of developing sources -- why put your friends out if you don't have to?

The most famous of the traditional sources of information about a person or group you are investigating is a person who feels he or she has gotten a rotten deal and is mad at your subject.

A few examples from my own experience should illustrate this point:

- *A man who lost an election in his union because the union leaders turned against him was suddenly eager to tell tales of corruption in his union to an outsider that he would never have discussed before the election that went bad.*
- *A man who was an accountant for a multi-million dollar political organization and was fired was willing not only to share copies of the organization's records, but was willing to reveal some facts very few people knew about a prominent state senator.*
- *A man who was a leader of one of the nation's largest Ku Klux Klan organizations and discovered that his boss apparently had more loyalty to lining his own pockets than to the cause of white supremacy. This contact was able to supply documents and personal information that would otherwise have been unavailable.*

The problem with developing these sources is, of course, finding them. Basically there are three ways of locating such sources: *1)* if you are lucky, during your homework you have found some group or individual that is suing your subject -- an excellent source indeed; *2)* your friendship network may be able to locate such a source; or *3)* if you have a solid reputation as an investigator who can not only uncover dirt but who can see to it that the dirt is either published or processed by the appropriate authorities, sources will come to you.

If you do have contact with a newspaper or magazine with a wide circulation, you can use it to help you to develop sources. It is a common journalistic practice to print some tantalizing bit of information about a subject in the hope that a potential source will read it and will call in, volunteering to help provide more information.

As a last resort, there is always the "going it cold" search for sources that may have information you can use about your subject. These are developed from the leads your chronology and organization profiles have given you. In going it cold, it is usually just a matter of perserverance in running down every possible lead you can until you finally find a source that can provide you with the evidence you need. Going it cold is not any fun, but sometimes it is the only technique that works.

Here's another area where your homework is critical. If you have developed any information at all that suggests that your subject has violated the law you may find that you can exchange your information for some help from law enforcement officials.

If you are going it cold, you should use your chronology and profiles to develop a list of possible sources that may be hostile to your subject. This is *Harry's Eleventh Law:* **Look for your subject's enemies.** Such people might include: former or current political opponents; organizations with a different position on issues than your subject; personal enemies; unhappy former employees; former spouses; and prosecuting attornies. When you're going it cold and interviewing former classmates, neighbors, or business associates, be sure that you try to elicit information about people who are "out to get" your subject.

Other Overlooked Sources

Aside from friendship networks, the most frequently overlooked pool of potential sources are people who like your subject or work for your subject. Your approach to this pool, of course, will be different from your approach to those in the "enemies" pool, a subject discussed in greater detail later in this manual.

And, for those investigators focusing in on businesses, there is one key person in every business who is probably the best source of information there is. The person has the same position in every organization. And the person is the single person who is most often overlooked by investigators. Have you guessed, from these clues, who I'm talking about? *The boss's secretary.* Secretaries are among the most difficult sources to develop because they usually genuinely like their bosses and because they have been selected for their position because they are known to be loyal to their bosses. Also, to some secretaries, the feeling of having -- and keeping -- secrets gives them a sense of importance that makes up for what are often very inequitable wages. But secretaries *can* be developed as sources. Just keep that in the back of your mind. I've only had luck with secretaries once. I was calling for an appointment with the company president and I noticed that the secretary seemed unusually agitated. I asked her if there was something wrong. She said, "Yes, they're shutting down the company". I had my exclusive before even the company's employees were told because by luck I had caught the secretary at a highly emotional and unguarded moment.

The second most important person in any company is the controller or the head accountant. Again, these people tend to be very tight-mouthed and extremely loyal. But it never hurts to be friendly to them. You never know when they may want to talk something over with you...

Harry's Twelfth Law: **Always be friendly to accountants and secretaries.**

CHAPTER 5
DOCUMENTS: YOUR GOLD MINE

Harry's Thirteenth Law: **Document everything you can.**

If you are following the dictates of Harry's Fourth and Fifth Laws in your investigations, you'll realize that one of the things you are really doing is "building a case". And even if the subject of your investigation turns out to be as clean as 19th Century arctic ice (almost impossible), you'll want to be able to prove it. To prove your facts to other people you will need to have evidence.

For our purposes, there are four sets of information investigators deal in:

1) documents obtained from public or private sources

2) things the investigator has personally heard or seen

3) things another person has personally heard or seen

4) third hand information

The fourth set of information is worthless in building a case. At best, it may be a source of leads to the other sets of information.

The first set of information generally makes the most convincing case.

Here's an example of a simple "case" that was built on documents alone:

> Only three documents were involved: *1)* a copy of an application to the IRS for tax exempt status; *2)* a copy of an annual statement of circulation to substantiate a second class mailing permit; and *3)* an internal organization newsletter.
>
> The subject of the investigation was a non-profit organization called Eagle Forum. The purpose of the investigation was to learn as much as possible about the organization's finances -- the documentary double-talk uncovered here was merely a bonus item.
>
> The IRS application made three statements: *1)* all members had to pay $2 dues; *2)* there were 40,000 members; and *3)* revenue from dues was less than $20,000. Actually, this single document was sufficient to prove that one or more of the three statements was untrue because if all 40,000 alleged members had paid the allegedly man-

datory dues, the organization's revenue from dues would have been $80,000.

An internal newsletter, what I call a semi-public document because it is available to some members of the public, made the statement that every member of Eagle Forum would receive a free subscription to a newsletter called the *Phyllis Schlafly Report*. If there were 40,000 members, then there would be at least that many copies of the report published.

The second-class mail permit annual filing (Statement of Ownership, Management and Circulation, Postal Service Form 3526) reported that only 15,000 copies of the *Report* during the time period referenced had been published each month.

These documents made the "case" stronger -- they were "second sources" that tended to show that the statements made in the IRS filing were not just an error in typing.

It should be noted that all that was technically proven in this "case" was that a spokesperson for Eagle Forum had made contradictory statements about the organization. What this proven fact meant was a matter of interpretation.

Most people I talked with interpreted the fact to mean that Eagle Forum was probably grossly exaggerating its size.

Because all of the "evidence" was in the form of documents, it was much more believable than any other kind of evidence would have been because the facts could be pointed out and everyone could see them for themselves. Also, documents were more convenient because they could be easily copied and shown to many people. (Interestingly, organizations that opposed the views expressed by Eagle Forum and Phyllis Schlafly never did anything with this information even though they had access to it. Apparently they felt it was to their advantage to continue to let the public believe that they were facing a strong and well-financed movement.) Incidentally, anyone who signs an application for exempt status with the IRS does so under penalty of perjury -- a law that is seldom enforced.

During the homework phase of your investigations you will often be rewarded with such bonuses as in the example above.

An investigator is not always fortunate enough to be able to build a case solely on public and semi-public documents and often has to rely on the second and third sets of information -- on what he/she has observed or what others have observed. In either situation, these sets of information should be documented. Many an investigation has fallen flat simply because the investigator did not do a good enough job when documenting this kind of information.

Here are two examples of documentation procedures:

1) Your own observations. Generally, you will find information from people either by talking to them on the phone, or by interviewing them, or by simply watching them in person. If you are on the phone, you should take notes of the conversation as it occurs. If the source is a friendly one you should ask if it is OK to tape the phone conversation so that you can quote statements accurately. If the source is hostile to you, you might not want to ask for permission to tape because a hostile source might simply hang up.

The tape or not-to-tape controversy is a major one among investigators. If you are using your own telephone it is perfectly legal for you to tape your conversations with anyone without telling them. The problem is that this type of evidence is often not admissable in court. Laws on taping conversations vary from state to state, change frequently, and become even more complex when you are using someone else's phone or if you are calling to a state different from your own. Those who argue against taping correctly note that good notes are all the evidence a court will require. Those who favor taping say that it is the only way to be sure that quotes are made accurately. Also, some investigators note, if you tell a source you have the statements on tape, that source won't be ready to lie about what he or she revealed when someone else asks for confirmation. My personal response to the taping controversy is that I am always ready to tape my phone conversations, but I only turn on the tape recorder when someone is admitting to an illegal act or when they are threatening me. Otherwise, in my book, the tape-recorder is too much trouble and discourages development of the best skill an investigator can have -- as nearly an infallible memory as possible.

In general, you should try to make complete notes while you are observing or listening. Then, immediately after you are done with the interview or period of observation, you should fill in your notes with *everything* you can remember, even if it does not seem important to you at the time. A few investigators have been known to take sloppy notes at the beginning, get half-way into their investigation and discover that they forgot to make a note of something they observed, and then -- a month or two after the interview or event -- try to reconstruct exactly what they saw or heard. This can ruin an otherwise perfectly sound investigation. Train yourself to make complete notes at the beginning.

If you know ahead of time that you will be seeing or hearing something that is very important to your "case", it is a good idea to take a witness with you. Then, after the observation or phone call, have your witness make independent notes of what he or she observed. Have the witness initial or sign the notes.

Any notes you make should always include this information:
- date and time of interview or observation
- the place and/or phone numbers used
- the names of all participants
- a description of the circumstances that might affect the accuracy of your report (example: "subject sat across table in a well-lit room")
- a note about when you actually made the notes

Once you develop a format for this information, stick to it so that recording it becomes a habit with you. The format I use is a simple one and you can see a sample on the next page. One thing you'll learn about note-taking: it's really only important that *you* can read your notes. Therefore you can use whatever form of personal shorthand that makes sense to you.

2) Someone else's observations. These fall into two groups: observations by a reporter that have been published, and observations by your source.

A word of caution about using newspaper reports as sources: don't trust what is printed. *If you're serious about using a newspaper report as part of your evidence package, you should do four things:*
- call the reporter who wrote the story and see if it was based on documents, or on what else
- try to verify the story independently
- ask the reporter if the publisher or anyone else is being sued for libel over the story (it is malicious libel if you base your

Sample Format For Notes

Phone interview X or field observation _____
Date of interview or observation: 2/22/80
Time of interview or observation: 4:30 PM Eastern
Name used for interview or observation: own
Location of interview or observation: home, call to 212-555-1212
Subject of interview or observation: fry. J.J. Jones preny. campaign
Names of other participants: None
Circumstances of interview or observation: call from self to J. Smith
When notes completed: during call

NOTES:

Q "How much $"
Smith: "raised 100K in Feb."
Q. where
Smith: "primarily New York state"
Q how
Smith: "Benefits with Looney Tunes Western gospel band"
Q where
Smith: "Biltmore"
Q. how many tickets
Smith: "10K"
Q price of tickets
Smith: "$10"
Q who put on show, how contact
Smith: manager is "Billy Bob at 202-555-1212"
Q. what cut he get
Smith: "I don't know."

Note to self— Smith got nervous near end. Something fishy?

own report on someone's articles that are the subject of a libel suit and it is gross negligence not to check to be sure there is no suit if you have any reason to suspect there might be one)
- make notes of your conversation and ask the reporter if he or she would send you copies of the pertinent documentary evidence.

As an example of reliability of newspaper reports, the *New York Times* once reported that a certain well-known arms dealer and soldier of fortune had been arrested on charges of dope smuggling but that the case was thrown out of court. Several other publications picked up on the *Times* version. On checking with the prosecuting attorney however, an investigator I know found out that charges hadn't been dropped at all and that the offense had been plea-bargained down to a misdemeanor. There is a big difference between having your case thrown out of court and plea-bargaining!

When you are dealing with an individual source who is helping you with your investigation, the source should have no qualms about being taped unless the source isn't playing square with you. Also, the source should be able to supply documents to substantiate his or her claims.

If your source is what might be called a "reliable" source, then the tape recording (which you will later transcribe) and any documents the source gives you should stand alone as evidence. But if you have any reason to suspect that your source may be hiding something or even lying to you, or if you think you will be handing your "case" over to a public attorney, then you should ask your source to sign an affidavit that says he or she is telling the full and complete truth, as best as she or he can recall it. The affidavit should include any information that will help make your source seem more credible to others -- describing what his/her position was with regard to the subject, how he/she came to know the information, and any special training he/she might have in observation and "objective" description -- former police officers, for example, have a high credibility rating in most courts. The affidavit should include the source's full name, any pseudonyms he or she may use, his or her current occupation, and his or her address and phone number. It should also include anything else you can get your source to volunteer -- social security number, drivers license number, etc. -- in case someone has to try to locate your source several months down the road. The affidavit should be notarized. The affidavit, of course, will describe the transcript of the interview, and you should have your source initial each page of the transcript.

That is an ideal situation. In the real world, most sources are somewhat afraid of retaliation from whomever they are informing you about and you are often lucky just to get a tape-recorded interview.

The best argument to convince a source to sign an affidavit is to be straightforward and say, "First, no one will believe that what you told me is true without an affidavit, and second, without something signed by you, I may not be able to use your information at all."

More On Documents

Earlier chapters have discussed some of the public documents available to you for your investigation and how to find out about others that probably exist. Before going on into semi-public documents and private documents, here is some more information about useful public documents.

Two wonderful public sources that often come in handy are the *Congressional Record* and printed records of hearings by committees and sub-committees of Congress.

Members of Congress are protected from libel suits in anything they say either on the floor of Congress or that they add to the *Congressional Record* in its "extension of remarks". This is sometimes useful to an investigator because as of this writing, if the investigator quotes from the *Congressional Record* the investigator is also libel-proof on the specific quote (whether or not the information is factual). Some members of Congress seem to have specific axes to sharpen and are ready to attack a variety of people and organizations as either terrorists, crooks, spies, communists, members of organized crime, or members of such groups as the Ku Klux Klan. Often, members will go out of their way to make sure that their information gets included in the *Congressional Record*. In fact, because members have fairly large salaried staffs and contacts in government that most of us do not have, much of their information, if used carefully, can be extremely valuable. So, when you're checking your library during your homework stage, look through indexes to the record for listings that may refer to your subject or your subject's affiliations. You may be pleasantly surprised by some Congressman blabbering that your subject is a kingpin in dope traffic, a communist, or whatever.

An even better source of information is records of Congressional hearings. This is one of the primary ways that journalists avoid being sued when they identify someone as being "linked to organized crime". The link they refer to was probably the testimony of a Department of Justice worker. Records of hearings have a very long life. For example, people are still getting away with statements like "identified as a member of the Communist Party", that are drawn from the McCarthy anti-communist hearings of some 30 years ago. Of course, there's no reason to believe that just because an FBI agent says someone was a communist that they were one, but it is useful background information for an investigator to have, especially if a second source can be found to confirm it. The record from the last round of the Kennedy-assassination hearings, for example, names a great many people as members of ultra-right organizations.

Finding the information you want from Congressional hearings can be a time-consuming process. Often copies of the reports are only available in federal archives (there are seven regional archive centers) which may mean a trip out of town. Even finding what reports have been printed can be tedious -- the best way I have found is to look at the monthly catalog of publications put out by the Government Printing Office. You can subscribe to the GPO catalog, but it'll be a lot cheaper for you if you find a library that subscribes.

What I generally do to avoid a lot of tedious work is to subscribe to the free monthly summary of GPO publications *(Selected U.S. Government Publications,* free from the Superintendent of Documents, Washington, DC 20402).When I see a report that sounds interesting to me, I order it (some reports sell out almost as fast as they are printed), read it, underline things that may be interesting to me in the future, and make notes of anything that is useful to any investigation I am currently involved in. My archives are full of copies of hearings and reports and I've been pleasantly surprised by what a good investment they have been.

For those of you who are into exposing what the federal government is up to, there is a third source that is invaluable and that is the the U.S. General Accounting Office. In 1975 the GAO made life easier for investigators by starting a monthly catalog of all of its reports, decisions, opinions, testimonies, and speeches. The reports you'll get from the GAO are by no means as exciting as some Congressional Hearings, but if you know what you're doing, they can be equally valuable. Unfortunately, the catalog takes an hour or so to go through. If you're too lazy to go to the library once a month to see what's new, you can subscribe to the catalog for $24 a year from the Superintendent of Documents. With very few exceptions the materials listed in the catalog are available free from the GAO. The catalog even includes a postage-paid request card. Or, if you like, you can call 202-275-6241. A lot of the reports on programs like *60 Minutes* are taken directly from GAO reports.

Another good source of specific information is special reports prepared by the Library of Congress for Congressional committees. These reports are generally accurate. One hint here: the reports are prepared by people who don't often get a great deal of acknowledgment for the work they've done. If you write to one of the authors of these reports asking for elaboration on a specific topic you may find that the researcher will be more than happy to help you (especially if you happen to mention that you are writing a book on the subject).

The Library of Congress can be useful for other things as well, especially for checking out who holds the copyright on books. An investigator researching the background of David Duke made excellent use of the Library of Congress to show that the Klan leader had probably authored a book for black militants and a book on sex. The Library of Congress copyright information provided the link between the two books and members of Duke's family. (Eventually, Duke admitted authoring the book for black militants. To my knowledge, no reporter has yet made the connection to the sex book.) One caution about the Library of Congress: if you want information fast, hire a researcher who can go there in person. Dealing by mail for requests on things like copyright checks can take months.

In addition to all of the above sources, most federal agencies author their own reports, many of which are available to the public. Usually these are published by the Government Printing Office and may be purchased.

By now you have probably gotten the point: the federal government provides a gold mine of information for the public investigator but it can be hard as hell to find what you want.

Your local college or university library, or major public library may be able to save you a lot of time if it subscribes to Congressional Information Service (CIS). If the government published it, CIS has probably indexed it and will, for a fee, send a researcher a copy of it. For information about CIS, write them at 7101 Wisconsin Ave., Suite 900, Washington, DC 20014 or call their publicity director at 301-654-1500. The publicity director may be able to tell you which local library subscribes to their service and save you a lot of calling.

All of that only scratches the top layer of dust off of the entire realm of useful public documents available to the citizen investigator. State governments publish their own materials. To my knowledge there is no simple way of finding out what has been published by any state except the one you live in unless you happen to have access to the Library of Congress. Getting copies of state documents can also be a chore, even within your own state. (If any reader has found a simple solution to this problem, please drop me a note care of the publisher.)

There are also dozens of useful directories, special indexes, and abstracts published by private firms that I haven't even mentioned here because they are the reference sources most people talk about. Two books listed in the resources section will give you all the details you need.

Semi-Public Documents

In this category I place materials that are not generally advertised. The most useful class of semi-public documents for the citizen investigator is probably corporations' annual reports. If the corporation sells stock on any of the exchanges regulated by the Securities Exchange Commission, these annual reports are a matter of public record and copies are filed with the SEC. Don't write to the SEC for copies though, write to the public relations director of the corporation itself. They are usually quite happy to send you whatever you want if they think their company will get some good publicity.

The second most useful class of semi-public documents for

the citizen investigator are newsletters published by various organizations. Some groups (usually not the ones you'll want to investigate) may send you complimentary copies of their magazine or newsletter. As to the others, you'll either have to join the organization, locate a member willing to share his/her copies with you, or locate a library that happens to have a subscription. Occasionally an organization that opposes your subject's positions may be willing to send you copies of the newsletters you're interested in. The Anti-Defamation League, for example, subscribes to every publication that it considers to be anti-Jewish (getting into their archives is another problem entirely). By contrast, any anti-Jewish or self-described "anti-Zionist" organization with any money at all will have archives of ADL literature (good luck getting access to these archives). Labor organizations keep track of anti-union activists, anti-union activists keep track of labor organizations, etc.

The third most useful class of semi-public documents is transcripts of trials. Generally, the transcripts are available only through the attorneys who handle the case. Theoretically, they are publicly available, but for the citizen investigator, it is easiest to go straight to the attorney and copy the parts you need. An even more interesting group of documents in this class is depositions taken by attorneys of witnesses on the opposing side. Much of the material in depositions, which are made under penalty of perjury, never sees the light of a courtroom because the information in them isn't particularly helpful to either side or because a trial judge rules that they are inadmissable as evidence. A general hint here, if you're dealing with attorneys at all in your investigation, is to be sure to ask them if there's anything interesting in the pre-trial depositions.

And Don't Forget

It's amazing how the simplest resources are often overlooked by investigators. In my experience, the most frequently overlooked public document is the telephone directory. More than just helping you to trace the address of a subject (or to learn that the subject isn't listed), a phone book can often lead you to other names that the subject is using. Reverse directories are better for this, but if you need information instantly, you can often get it out of the phone book or by making a call to an information operator.

CHAPTER 6
WHO ARE YOU... WHEN

There are two ways to go about an investigation -- the hard way and the easy way. I happen to value my time and energy a lot and so I always choose the easy way. I recommend it to you.

In order to make things easy for yourself, you have to make it as easy as possible for your sources -- whether they are public servants or private citizens -- to give you the information you want.

Depending on who you are and why you're doing your investigation, you may find that honesty about who you are and what you're up to is the best way to make people want to help you. Honesty is generally the easiest way out if you happen to be a well-known writer for a major, respected publication.

But if you're just J. Doe, public citizen, honesty will probably make things a lot tougher on you than they should be. To make things easier, you'll have to develop a "pretext" or cover story that will help your sources go out of their way to assist you and to give you what you want. You won't be alone at playing the pretext game -- lots of professional investigators and journalists do it all the time.

Playing the pretext game is perhaps one of the most entertaining parts of an investigation. It gives you a chance to act out many roles (author, oil dealer, minister -- anything except a law enforcement officer) you've always dreamt of playing.

Pretext interviews challenge your imagination and ingenuity. They test your knowledge of human nature and your ability to spin a good yarn.

Most people don't get (or make) the chance to play pretext. You may have been one of them up till now. Public reluctance to play pretext games works to your advantage when you decide to play because most people aren't paranoid about being approached by someone who isn't what they appear or pretend to be.

If playing pretext *is* foreign to you, here are two things you should practice with: *1)* answering your phone and telling people you're not in; and *2)* applying for jobs you're totally unqualified for, making up employment histories to suit the job. (Anyone who's been down-and-out probably already has a perfect background for the pretext game.)

As you practice with pretexts, you'll be amazed at how willing most people are to believe your stories.

Here's one of the wildest examples of a pretext game that I've run across:

A woman I know had conveniently left some bad debts in Virginia and moved to Hawaii. She was equipped with a fake drivers license from Moose Jaw, Canada. She picked Moose Jaw as her last residence because she didn't think anyone in the Aloha State would pay the trans-Pacific phone bill to check out her non-existent background there. The state accepted her ID and gave her a new drivers license, banks accepted it, and most creditors accepted it. After a few months in Hawaii she applied for a car loan. In two days the credit manager asked her to come to his office to give him more information to complete her application. Fortunately for her, the address she had selected in Moose Jaw actually existed -- the credit manager had checked it out! In fact, she had picked the address from a directory of Russian Orthodox churches. As it turned out, no one at the church spoke English well enough to give the credit people the information they needed, so the credit manager asked my friend, "Why don't you have a credit history and what were you doing living at a Russian Orthodox church?" She began weaving a wonderful story. It was so interesting that the company president and a secretary came in to listen to it. She had ended an unhappy marriage ten years ago, she told them. Depressed and bewildered, she had decided she would become a nun. A friend recommended that she spend some time at the nunnery (non-existent) at the Moose Jaw church (whose name she remembered). My friend's audience believed her and began to question her about what life was like in a Russian Orthodox nunnery. She spent an hour describing the details of her nonexistent experience at the non-existent monastary. "We spent several hours each day gardening..."; "Yes, it was interesting living in such a strange environment, especially when I wasn't Russian...". The loan was approved.

My friend's experience illustrates a few basics of using a pretext: *1)* start with a grain of truth (the address and church were real); *2)* fit the story to your age and gender (had she been a man she would have been a monk); *3)* talk about things you are familiar with (gardening); *4)* tell the listener a story that turns him/her on; *5)* sometimes the most outrageous pretexts are more believable than the truth.

In practical terms, you should analyze the person or agency you want information from. Ask yourself who the source is most used to giving information to, or who would the source be most eager to give information to. Here are a few examples:

People who are angry .... Sympathetic "crusaders"
Personnel managers . Credit department, employers
Most public officials .... Newspaper reporters
Real estate agents .... Home buyers
Reporters .... Other reporters
Academic "experts" ...... Students, other "experts"
Occult practitioners ..... Other occult practitioners
Dope dealers .... Dope buyers & distributers
Public prosecutors ... Reporters, other prosecutors
Etc. ...

Most often, your source won't check your pretext. If you are dealing with sources who are a bit paranoid, information in the chapter on infiltration will be more relevant than the simple pretext game.

After having decided who you are, brush up on whatever jargon and information you are supposed to know, get a sense of how to use your cover to get the specific information you want, and go to it. Have fun, and remember *Harry's Fourteenth Law:* **Make things easy on yourself by making things easy for your sources.**

CHAPTER 7
INTERVIEWING TECHNIQUES

Harry's Fifteenth Law: **Before beginning an interview, be thoroughly prepared.**

One of the most frequent mistakes made by novice investigators is not preparing well enough for an interview with a source. It's a trap that even experienced investigators can fall into when they're paying too much attention to their pretext, or when they're over-excited because they finally have located the perfect source of information about a subject.

Go into every interview, even the most casual phone call, totally prepared with a list of all the information you want to get. Tell yourself that this particular interview, this particular call, may be the only time you will ever be able to talk to this specific source.

If you're using a pretext, you should be sure you are comfortable with it and that you can carry it on throughout the conversation. Some people, myself included, make brief notes about the pretext they're using not only to help stay on track during the interview, but as an aide to remembering which pretext has been used with whom. Whether you make a note of your pretext or not, you should have your pretext down so well that you don't have to think about it and so that it doesn't get in the way of your most important job -- getting information.

Before preparing your interview you should make yourself familiar with whatever information you have about your source and try to anticipate his or her response to you.

You should prepare your interview in writing. You should phrase three or four different questions to cover each piece of data you want to elicit. If you are doing a phone interview, keep the questions in front of you and check them off as you get answers to them. If you're doing an interview in person, try to develop a pretext that will allow you to take your notes with you.

Check your interview questions over carefully. Do you know what you *specifically* want the source to tell you? Have you formulated three or four different ways of getting the information? Have you made questions to cover every piece of information you want?

After completing this part of your interview preparation, you should add some questions designed to make your source comfortable, what I call "throw-away questions". Also, you should be sure to have some leading and open-ended questions that will give your source a chance to tell you more than you want. You can also add extra questions about things you think your source might know -- for example, other people who can confirm what your source says.

It's a good idea, once you've written out your interview, to rehearse it in your mind, trying to anticipate your source's responses and trying to work your questions in so that they don't interrupt or even stop the flow of the interview.

Rehearsing for interviews might sound primitive, but you can never be too prepared. I've been doing interviews for two decades and I still mentally go over each interview before picking up the phone or leaving the car. The reason for this is simple: sources are not always easy to come by and it's simpler to make sure you have your interview prepared than to be caught forgetting something and then finding you have to develop another source to get that bit of information you could have had so simply on your first try.

One final point: Try, during the course of an interview, to get your source to agree to talk with you again in case you need more information. That way, in case you have forgotten something, you may be covered.

Interviews are always different from each other, so it's difficult to give more guidelines than those given above. The better you are prepared, the less nervous you will appear and the more energy you will be able to devote to *listening* to your source.

Another hint: When you're listening, listen for the blank spaces -- the areas that the source doesn't want to talk about. Often, what a source doesn't say can be a good source of future leads and give you an insight into what is going on.

Another pitfall to avoid: Many novice investigators, desperate to make their sources comfortable, will suggest that if the source is uncomfortable that his or her remarks be kept "off the record". By common agreement, "off the record" means that you cannot print the information you learn from that source and that you will have to get some other source to tell you the information. *Don't.* Why put limits on yourself before you even know what the source is going to tell you? Why put ideas into your source's head that will help him or her, but *hurt* your investigation?

Often, a source will conclude an interview, after realizing what type of information has been released, by saying "and that was off the record". Also by common practice, if something is to be off the record, the source must say so *before* giving you the information.

Sometimes, when a source tells you information should be kept "off the record", what the source is really trying to say is that it is OK to use the information, but not to use his or her name. Check to see if that is what your source means -- in journalese it's "not for attribution". As best you can, keep from making an "off the record" agreement. One way around this might be, during the interview simply ask the source, for the record, if such and so is true. All the source has to do then is to say yes or no -- sometimes a great deal easier than to answer a question straightforwardly.

Occasionally you may run into another type of journalistic agreement, most often proferred by politicians -- that certain information be treated only as "background" or "deep background". What this means is that you are agreeing to listen to something but not to let anyone know that you know it. This kind of agreement is most often honored in the breach. In a few months both you and the source will probably forget that it was conditioned on a "background" agreement and you can begin asking other people if they've heard about the information.

One hint about interviews that might sound redundant: know ahead of time *exactly* what you want your source to say and prepare your series of questions to lead your source into saying precisely what you want. There are a variety of responses that you can get from any source on a specific item of information. The most common example is getting a source to confirm or deny your information. Before going after this type of response, know exactly what you want: Do you want an explicit denial of every detail? A denial of only one of many details? A "refuse to comment" that looks incriminating? A yes or no answer, or an explanation? Conformation of a specific act? What kind of confirmation -- did the source see it, participate in it, or just hear about it?

Also, before going into an interview, you should know whether you are going to leave the source friendly or hostile to you. In general, as you arrange interviews for your research, it is best to leave the people that are going to be hostile until last -- you can be fairly certain they won't talk to you again, so save these for the finishing touches on your investigative project.

It is always a good idea to give the subject of your interview a chance to deny or to explain the facts you have uncovered. If your facts are conclusive enough, it doesn't matter what your subject says. However, if the subject can be trapped into admitting that what you've found is true by getting the chance to explain it to you, let your subject do so.

Subject interviews, when you do them, are *always* last in your investigation.

I've dealt with sources who simply answered my questions directly and without difficulty -- sometimes out of shock, but most often because they wanted to help. Other sources have talked for hours over several days before finally answering the specific question I wanted answered. Some sources I've had to trick into giving me information. Other sources I've had to shout into giving me information. I've sat and listened to the most boring stories from sources simply waiting for a way to get my questions in in a way that didn't interrupt the interview and make the source clam up. With some sources I've been genuinely friendly. With others I've had to fake being friendly. With others I've had to fake being mad.

There are as many interview styles as there are interviews and interviewers. Every interviewer should develop a number of styles.

Here are some "case histories" from my own files:

> **Purpose of call:** *get subject's unlisted number*
> **Pretext:** *old school friend of subject*
> **Call to:** *person believed to be current friend of subject*
> **Results:** *half hour of "reminiscenses" covering information I already knew, then phone number given. The phone number led to locating the subject's address*

> **Purpose of call:** *get phone number of Los Angeles US Labor Party Office*
> **Pretext:** *interested public citizen from L.A.*

76

Call to: *Detroit anti-drug coalition*
Results: *after a hustle for donations, phone number was given. And an extra bonus -- the name of the Los Angeles head*

※※※

Purpose of call: *get US Labor Party spokesman to admit to certain activities that may have violated federal elections laws*
Pretext: *none*
Calls to: *Los Angeles chief, New York spokesman*
Results: *Los Angeles chief refused to talk. Learned name of second-in-command. LA hangs up. Half hour lecture on evils of media by NY spokesman. Accidentally confirms suspected violation of law. When returned to topic he waffled.*

※※※

Purpose of call: *to determine if United Klans of America active in Boston*
Pretext: *none*
Call to: *Robert Shelton, UKA head*
Results: *in answers to question on women's auxiliary, he notes that they are active in Boston*

※※※

Purpose: *determine economic state of subject company*
Pretext: *friend of supervising employee*
Interview: *developed during five-weeks' mutual participation in local bowling league*
Results: *supervisor warns of layoffs pending, planned cutbacks in hours*

※※※

Purpose: *determine if subject had had recent contact with Weather Underground*
Pretext: *interview about FBI harassment*
Interview: *eight hours on each of three days*
Results: *established that probably had no contact*

※※※

Purpose: *to determine if subject company reports names of clients to FBI or local police*
Pretext: *wish to become employee*
Interview: *half hour plus thirty-minute tour of company*

Results: *tour showed that this practice was not current -- procedures described do not elicit names of customers*

⁂ ⁂ ⁂

Purpose: *to determine if a business is making payoffs to criminals for "protection"*
Pretext: *manager of similar business, new to town*
Interview: *several contacts over several week period*
Results: *currently making payoffs, bonus: name of collector*

⁂ ⁂ ⁂

Purpose: *to determine if subject doctor illegally prescribing controlled substances*
Pretext: *patient referred by another patient*
Interview: *one visit to office*
Results: *talks with patients in waiting room showed they knew the doctor freely prescribed uppers. Received medically unrequired prescription for controlled substance without physical examination.*

⁂ ⁂ ⁂

Remember, every interview is important. If you blow one, even an innocuous one, you're making more work for yourself. You can control most interviews and will get the information you want only if you know exactly what it is you want and if you are thoroughly prepared.

CHAPTER 8
INFILTRATION

When the information you need is held by a group that is a clandestine organization, or even just a private organization that simply wants to maintain its privacy, sometimes the only way to access the information is to infiltrate the group.

This investigative procedure is only infrequently used by "journalists" working with the established press. At times it is the most productive procedure to use. It is also potentially the most dangerous even though the real dangers may be only to one's own level of paranoia.

There are basically four types of infiltration:

1) by telephone
2) by mail
3) in person
4) by creating a vehicle designed to draw the organization's members into a business or group controlled by the investigator

Each type of infiltration is progressively more dangerous.

If you are doing the investigation for the purpose of publishing it, certain laws may preclude you from using the information obtained by your own infiltration actions -- most notably, you may be sued for violation of privacy or harassment.

No matter what you intend to do with the information, you should first try to develop your "case" by the methods described earlier in this manual. Before beginning an in-person penetration or developing a covert front of your own, be certain that you have exhausted every other avenue of investigation open to you. In most cases direct infiltration is neither desireable nor required. It is also nerve-wracking.

Infiltration By Phone

This is probably the safest type of infiltration and the most innocuous. In fact, it is similar to the procedure of making "pretext" calls.

The difference between the simple "pretext" call and the infiltration call is that your "pretext" in an infiltration is the desire to support the activities of your subject organization or to join it. At this level of infiltration you won't be given access to all of the group's darkest secrets, but the information you do get may be just what you need to finish your "case".

During an infiltration by phone operation, as in any infiltration operation, do not give your true name or disclose any accurate information about yourself. You may be asked for a phone number. If you do not have a second phone that is listed to someone other than yourself (a good investment for the investigator who finds that she or he will be doing a great many infiltrations), then I suggest that you give the phone number of a telephone booth. This way the organization may believe you are sincere (because you gave a phone number) and if it tries to call you will generally get a busy signal or no answer at all. At this level, the organization will probably not bother to check out the telephone and you are spared possible future phone harassment. It also means that you are in control of contacts with the organization.

You will doubtlessly be asked for an address. Again, a good investment is a Post Office box that is not readily traceable to you. You may be pressed for a street address, so you will have to say that you travel and don't have a permanent residence. Give an "emergency" address -- a street number of your local phone company or other favorite agency (don't give a private party's address -- why spread whatever potential harassment you might someday face to innocent people?).

A general hint on making Post Office boxes less traceable: almost anyone can, if they want to, learn the name of a boxholder, even over the phone -- as we have seen in an earlier chapter. So why put the box in your, or anyone else's, name? If the box is held in the name of a business or organization it will be that much more difficult to trace to you -- especially if the business or organization has filed its "dba" in a county different from the county that the post office box is in. An alternative is simply to put the box in one of your "cover" names, a maneuver that more-or-less depends on how lax your local post office is, or how much time you want to invest in documenting a cover name well enough for your post office to accept.

Other investigators have recommended mail-forwarding services. I personally prefer not to use these because it is sometimes very easy to find out information about the user of a mail-forwarding service from the service's operator. It is especially easy for police and postal-inspector types. Of course, one could conceivably construct a relatively impenetrable series of mail-forwarding "drops", with the last one being in another country. I just like the post office box because it is more convenient and less expensive.

A second type of infiltration by phone is also similar to the pretext call. Depending on the organization's paranoia or internal security measures, it can also be valuable for learning certain information about an organization. In this infiltration technique the investigator pretends he or she has just moved to the area and was, a couple of years ago, a member of the group in another state. If you have enough information to develop a story to cover your membership in another state -- names of members there, the kinds of things the group did, etc. -- you will often be able to pick up data on your "local" group in one simple phone call. Since long distance calls no longer sound like they're long distance and are often more clear than cross-town calls, you can repeat the same technique to learn about chapters of your organization in a variety of places.

Generally, infiltration by phone is used only to find out names of organization leaders, addresses, and phone numbers. You may possibly learn about a few past activities and whatever's planned for the immediate future.

Infiltration by phone is also generally a one-time venture.

Infiltration By Mail

Infiltration by mail is similar to infiltration by phone. You need a phony name and a safe address. Your purpose is simply to get access to an organization's internal literature. A secondary purpose may be to see if the organization is giving or renting its mailing list to another group. If the second type of information is what you're looking for, then I suggest using a different name for each organization you plan to mail to. Simple variations of the same name are also adequate, for example: Arthur Harry, B. Harry, C. Harry, Mrs. J. Harry, etc. (Be sure to keep a record of what name you've given to which group.)

I would venture to guess that the vast majority of information about private groups and organizations has been developed, over the years, by simply reading the group's own literature very carefully.

Most organizations recognize that their newsletters, etc. are easily susceptible to mail infiltration and save their most important information for personal or telephone transmission. Nevertheless, an organization is often totally unwilling to release *any* information to "strangers" -- even what it has already published in its own literature.

It is genuinely amazing what information can be gathered from reading a year's worth of internal newsletters. This includes, but is not limited to:
- *names of the group's leaders, as well as chapter leaders*
- *the cities the leaders are active in*
- *names and locations of supporters*
- *related activities the organization supports (publishing ventures, political groups, etc.)*
- *dates and locations of meetings and other organization events*

The internal newsletters may also make statements about membership and finances. These, I have found, are generally lies, put there either to give an impression of greater strength than actually exists, or as a way of soliciting more money.

Other information can be found simply from noting the return address used on the group's envelopes, and from any postal permit they may use.

Infiltration by mail is one of the most common activities going on today. In general, any organization can expect that for every thousand copies of newsletters it mails, five, if not more, are being sent to people who have infiltrated the group by mail.

Infiltration by mail can also include buying a share of stock in an organization that is not publicly traded just for the purpose of getting a copy of the company's annual report. In this sense, infiltration by mail is a generally accepted practice.

Another version of infiltration by mail is developing a correspondence with a member of an organization. Some organizations seem dominated by compulsive letter-writers. If they think you share their views and that they can help you to be more effective at promoting these views, such correspondents may be quite willing to write to you. Much organizational work is accomplished by correspondence nets. If you can plug in, so much the better for you. Eventually, of course, one of the people you're writing to or one of their friends, will want to meet you in person. If you don't follow through, your mail-cover has been blown.

Infiltration by mail... a political organization backed by a local Ku Klux Klan group.

There's another difficulty about this kind of mail infiltration, especially if you expect to write about the organization: the person who generates a letter is, by common law, the owner of the copyright to that letter. You may not lawfully, therefore, quote from it directly or publish it. You can take some comfort from the fact that this law is generally ignored because the letter-writer probably doesn't want the further embarassment that a public trial could bring.

Infiltration by mail is usually safe and is a very inexpensive way to get a great deal of information you wouldn't get any other way.

Just one caution: don't pay by check or credit card. Always transact in cash or money order. Again, the point is to learn about the organization, not to give the group tools to learn more about you.

Direct Infiltration

To those who have read too many spy novels, or who have very active imaginations, direct infiltration of a subject organization may sound exciting, glamorous, and even fun.

It is definitely none of the above. Think about it for a minute: if you join an organization you will eventually be forced to demonstrate by your own actions that you support the group's philosophy. Theoretically, if you're investigating the group, you really don't accept its goals (or else you wouldn't want to expose them). Having to act out things that run contrary to your own philosophy can do dreadful things to your psyche.

Nonetheless, direct infiltration is sometimes the only way you will get the information you want.

There are two types of direct infiltration: *short-term* and *long-term*. The investigator is advised *against* undertaking a long-term infiltration for a variety of reasons: *1)* it is harmful to your mental/spiritual health; *2)* the longer you expose yourself the greater chance you stand of being exposed; *3)* it's usually cheaper and easier to develop the friendship of a member and get him or her to "defect" and tell you everything and more than you could learn by direct infiltration. In addition to this, any organization that is worth a long-term infiltration usually has several ranks of initiates arranged in some sort of hierarchy. It may take you years to get to the top -- if you get there at all. Low-ranked members of any serious organization are never

Infiltration is all around us.

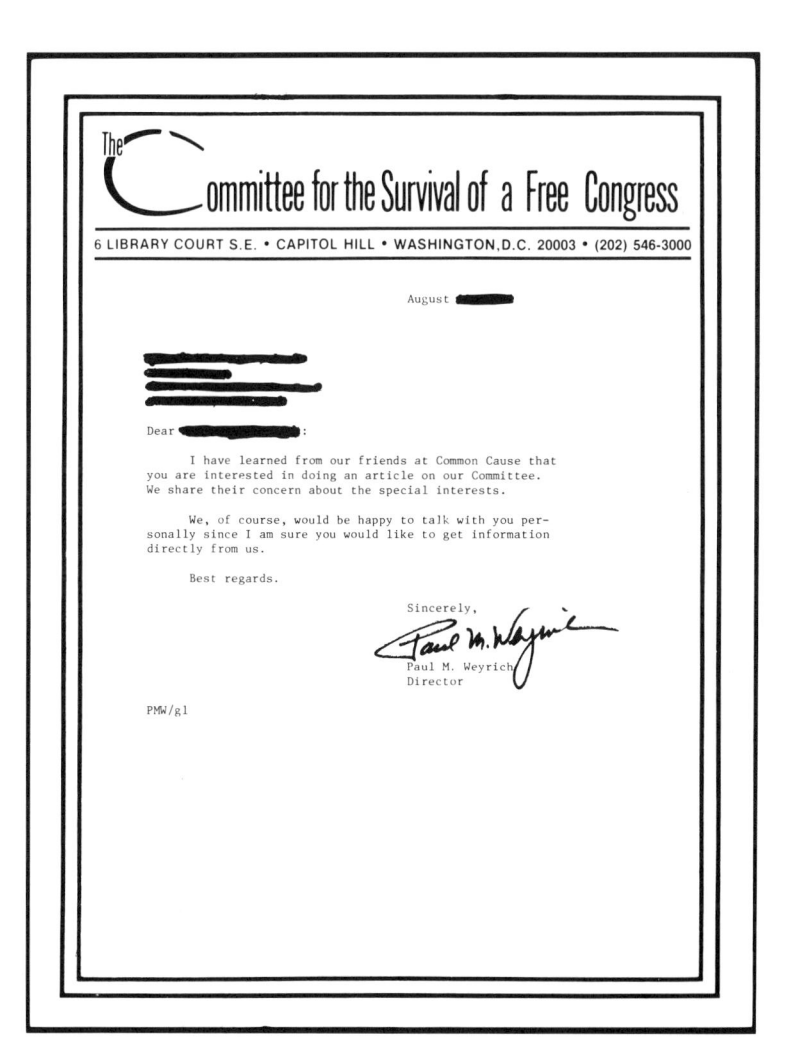

The Committee for the Survival of a Free Congress

6 LIBRARY COURT S.E. • CAPITOL HILL • WASHINGTON, D.C. 20003 • (202) 546-3000

August ▮▮▮

▮▮▮▮▮
▮▮▮▮▮
▮▮▮▮▮

Dear ▮▮▮▮▮:

    I have learned from our friends at Common Cause that you are interested in doing an article on our Committee. We share their concern about the special interests.

    We, of course, would be happy to talk with you personally since I am sure you would like to get information directly from us.

    Best regards.

Sincerely,

Paul M. Weyrich
Paul M. Weyrich
Director

PMW/gl

given the complete story about their group's operations.

For these reasons I advise that you *never* undertake a long-term infiltration and that you restrict your James Bond fervor to short-term infiltrations.

Harry's Sixteenth Law: **Never take any risk that you can avoid.**

Before undertaking a short-term infiltration, you should analyze what benefits you expect to get beyond those you could get from a regular investigation or from phone or mail infiltration.

Generally, the purposes of a short-term infiltration include:
1) getting information that goes beyond what the group has printed -- especially the names of local contacts
2) getting a better feel for the group
3) talking with members (or employees) who've been involved longer than you have, to get more information about local activities and background on local leaders
4) hoping that you will observe or hear that bit of evidence that will help to complete your "case"

Additionally, you may have the bonus of getting literature (documentation) that you did not get through your mail infiltration.

A direct infiltration is usually undertaken after an infiltration by mail or phone. The reason for this is that to be successful at a direct infiltration you must already have a good grip on the group's philosophies, what kind of members it attracts, and what kind of special jargon members tend to use: in other words, you'll have to establish a "cover" for yourself.

Before beginning a short-term infiltration you should already have planned certain basics about how you intend to appear as a genuine convert. As I like to say, you should prepare to be as inconspicuously conspicuous as possible. You should have an idea of the kinds of clothes members are likely to wear and should outfit yourself accordingly. Some writers may advise a "disguise" for short-term infiltrations. I have found that this isn't really necessary. Blending into the crowd is the best disguise there is. Also, it's convenient to wear some kind of pin or insignia from a group that your subject organization is in sympathy with. The purpose of this is to focus attention on your insignia, rather than on the details of your appearance. With any luck you'll be remembered as the person who "wore that Jesus

First pin", or that "red star", and not as "that five-foot-ten guy with wavy blonde hair who had a mole on his left cheek".

Other slight changes in your normal mode of behavior will also help people who might later want to identify you to become confused: if you smoke, don't; if you don't wear glasses, do; if you're twenty, try to look 28; and so on.

Your research prior to a direct penetration should help you to develop a good cover story. It's always a good idea to be new to the area -- just be prepared to give complete details about the place you supposedly moved from; a line of work different from your own is good cover, too; just know what you're talking about. You should be pretty familiar with the causes advocated by the organization and how they were fought for in the geographic area you say you are from. It's also a good idea to know what kind of literature, other than the group's own, members are likely to read. Then you can swap stories you've read in that source.

If you have a unique accent that will make you stick out from the crowd, get rid of it.

When you go to the meeting of the group you plan to infiltrate, come prepared with some spare cash (but not so much as to make you conspicuous). Organization leaders often measure loyalty in terms of cash contributions.

Developing a "cover" as described above is similar to developing a pretext. The rules are the same -- try to find a story that in some way suits your personality, that has at least a bit of factual basis, and that you can talk about comfortably.

And, when you finally get to the meeting or function, don't make yourself conspicuous by asking a lot of questions. With a good set of ears and simply by being a casual conversationalist, you'll probably get all the information you need. If you need more information after the first event, you can ask questions at the second event -- after you've learned how to phrase them so they don't seem strange or suspicious.

When you've obtained the information and documentation you need, stop your penetration and move your cover person to another state.

A word about cover names -- for some people (myself included), it is somehow difficult to remember your cover name when someone asks you. As an aide to my own memory, I choose a cover name that somehow relates to either the name of the organization, the goals of the organization, or to one of its leaders. For Nazi penetrations you might try something Germanic. For Communist penetrations you might try something Eastern-European or upper-crust New York. Whatever clue works for you -- it's very embarassing to suddenly not remember your own name (although it's quite alright to have trouble with your phone number -- many people do).

Personally, the only benefit I've ever received from short-term infiltrations has not been in terms of hard data or incriminating evidence, although names and addreses of everyone you can get are bound to come in useful sometime. My short-term infiltrations are primarily done so that I get a feeling for the style and personality of the organization. Mail infiltration may give me the idea that a group is very large and very wealthy. A direct infiltration may turn up evidence that the opposite is true. As a bonus to my short-term investigations I am careful to note the names of any people one would not normally expect to be at a meeting of the group. In organizations that are devoted to electoral politics more can be seen from who comes and who doesn't come to a dinner or meeting than from all of the group's posturings and statements.

Also, a direct infiltration may show that an organization you thought was violence-prone is really a peace-loving group.

There's nothing like seeing things first-hand when you're in search of facts -- something a great many reporters seem to forget quite often.

Indirect Infiltration

This infiltration technique will rarely be used by the citizen investigator. It is included here, however, because it has been used by public investigators and can be useful as a means of obtaining some information.

What is involved is setting up an organization whose primary purpose is to recruit members from a subject organization. These new recruits can be used to provide information about the subject organization.

Your covert organization can be something as simple as a newsletter, as expensive as a book store designed to appeal to members of your subject organization, a phony firm designed to entrap the subject in an illegal transaction, or simply a book or other appealing item that is sold to members of a subject organization and their sympathizers for the simple purpose of developing a list of names and addresses and whatever information can be elicited from the checks you receive in the mail.

In this type of operation it is very easy to overstep the bounds of investigating and into the unethical area of provocation. In general, if your purpose is entrapment of someone in an illegal act, you should check out your activities with law-enforcement types -- no reason for you to be arrested along with your subjects.

The newsletter operation is perhaps the easiest -- just run up a few press releases announcing the publication and send them to publications that are read by members of your subject organizations. It is advisable to actually publish a few issues. Another advantage of a newsletter is that you can exchange copies of it for the newsletters of other organizations. If you are studying an entire array of organizations, this is sometimes a cost-effective method of mail infiltration.

One caution here as with any operation that involves you *receiving* money: be scrupulously honest about your financial treatment of your patrons. If you cannot deliver your product, return peoples' money! Anything less is mail fraud and can set you up for several months free room and board at a federal prison.

About five years ago I used the newsletter ploy quite usefully. I've never used the techniques described below, but I know people who have:

>About fifteen years ago an acquaintance of mine set up a book store to attract patrons who belonged to subject organizations. The bookstore became quite a social gathering place and the bookstore operator was able to pick up a lot of inside information.
>
>David Duke, head of a Ku Klux Klan outfit, sold a book on black militancy. Its purpose, he later told reporters, was so that his organization could develop a list of names and addresses of black militants.

Other efforts I'm familiar with go beyond information-gathering into attempts to subvert subject organizations. One of the smaller Watergate scandals, for example, was the fact that the Nixon re-election effort, fearing that a strong third-party vote would hurt Nixon's chances for re-election, sent a contribution to an American Nazi organization so that the Nazis could disrupt local third-party efforts. And, by now, everyone is probably aware that the FBI set up dummy Klan groups during the late 60's and early 70's. Even today, in both left wing and right wing circles, various camps continually charge that someone (either the Soviets, Jews, leftists, or certain right-wing groups) are running front organizations for the purpose of information gathering and subversion. I've never seen anything that presented hard proof of these allegations. Maybe if some reader has proof, he or she could forward it to me -- it's one story I've always wanted to run down.

If all of the operations described in this chapter sound like topics in an FBI manual, they probably are. It's up to you if you need, or want, to use any of them. If you do, remember that no organization takes kindly to infiltrators of any sort.

CHAPTER 9
SPECIAL SOURCES

There are three types of common sources that demand special attention: 1) professional informers; 2) police; and 3) politicians.

As with any serious source, you should evaluate them all in terms of the fact that each of them is talking to you out of their own self-interest. Each wants you to *do* something. Everything is fine if your self-interest at the moment happens to coincide with that of your source. But when they conflict, things may get a bit complicated. As you interview your source you should be aware of what type of axe they are trying to grind. This will help you to evaluate the credibility of their information.

Professional Informers

There are fundamentally two types of professional informers: those who are directed by someone to penetrate an organization, and those who are recruited from within their organization to report on it. Most often both sorts of informers are usually paid by one police agency or another. On occasion, professional informers make a career out of selling information to whomever will buy.

The professional informer who has been directed and paid to infiltrate and report on an organization is generally more reliable and more objective than a recruit from within. The explanation for this is quite simple. The recruit from within an organization had originally been converted to the organization's goals. Along with this conversion process the recruit developed an intense loyalty to his or her comrades. The process of then abandoning the group and finking on comrades is spiritually and psychologically shocking. Additionally, the new recruit generally finds he or she has to go out of his/her way to prove loyalty to his/her new masters -- the police or other control person. As you can imagine, this process does not make for a high level of emotional or mental stability.

Most often, the investigator will "meet" the professional informer only through the data supplied by his or her superiors. Occasionally, however, the professional informer will find his or her way to the investigator and directly supply information.

It is this type of source that is the most suspect. Generally, this source is motivated by the fact that he or she believes that the agency that has paid for information has not dealt fairly with him or her. In fact, that is often the case. Many police agencies value informers only for the information they produce. Any sympathy for their personal problems is often only superficial. When the police agency no longer wants or needs the kind of information the source can provide, he or she is most often tossed out cold without even a thank-you. Add this to the fact that most informers are paid very little for their information, or have been forced to inform in exchange for being "let off" from one or another criminal charge, and you have the makings of a complete mental collapse. It's a pattern most stable people can't take: betray friends for new "friend" or cause; be betrayed by new "friend" or cause.

A source who's been left out in the cold is generally motivated by one of two (or both) desires: a need to find someone who needs him/her and will befriend him/her; a desire to exact a pound of flesh from the agency that turned him/her out into the cold.

These motivations pose some major problems for the investigator, not the least of which is that the source will try to please the investigator by giving him/her whatever information the investigator seems to want to hear, even if it is not true. In addition, in order to develop this type of source, the investigator generally has to extend a certain amount of friendship and sympathy, even if it is not real. This process then begins a vicious cycle: the source, finding a "real" friend, is again emotionally uplifted as he/she is brought out from the cold; the investigator, once the investigation is completed, generally wants to drop involvement with the source -- again kicking the source out into the cold.

My experience with this type of source has been profitable in terms of the information received because such sources usually provide documents -- either from the organization they've finked on, or from their dealings with police agencies; but has been painful emotionally. Such sources, I've found, tend to cling, trying to reestablish the "friendship" they've lost with you. You may find yourself continually hounded by the one-time source and it may be difficult to sever the relationship.

After three rounds with three different sources of this type I've personally decided that it's generally not worth the emotional hassle for me to deal with them.

One caution for you: be aware of this type of source's motivations, and make doubly sure that this type of source provides documents to support his or her claims.

Police Sources

The only access you are likely to have to a professional informer who is still on the payroll is through the summaries of information that his/her police bosses supply to you. This saves you the trouble of dealing with informants directly, but you have no way of assessing the informant's reliability. The police (also FBI, BATF, CIA, etc.) will tell you how reliable *they* think the informant is, but their statements about reliability must be weighed against the obvious self-interest police have in keeping only "reliable" informants on the payroll. Their standards of reliability may be totally opposite from yours.

Police agencies, of course, are good for much more than the information they obtain through their informants. Police agencies can provide you with any criminal records your subject or his/her associates may have with relative ease. *And,* they can access this information nation-wide.

As you can see, police agencies can be one of the best sources of information an investigator can access. But again we must examine motivation. Police agencies simply don't go around handing out free rap sheets. In many instances it is against the law for them to do so. John or Jane Smith, public citizen, may ask a dozen times and will never get a rundown from a police agency on anything or anyone.

However, police agencies have learned that some investigators tend to dig up information that will help them with their own investigations. It is sometimes possible, when you and the police happen to be working on the same investigation, to trade information. Generally, they'll want a look at the quality of *your* goods first, however.

In my own experience, I have only made good contacts with police agencies when we were pursuing the same investigation. Generally I gave more information than I got, but what I did get would have been nearly impossible to get anywhere else.

Some individuals I know, however, have sustained long-term relationships with police agencies and can get practically anything they want anytime they want. This type of relationship is common between reporters who have been on the "police beat" for several years and who have developed a genuine friendship with one or more officers. Either wittingly or unwittingly, these reporters have made a trade-off for their access to information: they are intensely loyal to their friends in the agencies they deal with and generally take everything the police tell them as gospel truth. Unless you happen to be religious, you know that no one has their hands on absolute truth. Such reporters tend to face an unmanageable conflict of interest if, for example, they are called upon to investigate police brutality.

There are ways to access police information without needing a direct contact with any police agency. One of the best of these methods is described below.

The Policician As A Source

If you remember the chapter on developing "inside" sources, you may recall a type of source who is a "sociometric star". The sociometric star is someone who knows a great many people from a diversity of backgrounds. Such sociometric stars are the best sources to cultivate, and among the best sociometric stars you can find are politicians.

Politicians, by virtue of their jobs, need to know and have access to hundreds of people, even thousands. Contacts are needed to raise money for campaigns. And once in office, contacts are needed to get legislation passed. When contacts aren't initiated by the politician, there are dozens of lobbyists initiating contact on their own, and politicians generally try not to alienate anyone. In the politics of the possible, it's best not to make any serious enemies. Additionally, most public agencies depend on the politician's vote for their appropriations. Therefore, representatives of these agencies work hard to keep politicians happy. Among agencies requiring budget approval, of course, are police agencies. You might be surprised how easy it is for a politician to get rap sheets and reports from police agencies.

And, there's an added bonus that comes along with politicians that makes them my favorite sources: politicians pick up a lot of gossip -- who's sleeping with whom, who's being bought by what group, etc. This kind of gossip is not only fun, it's a great source of leads for investigations. I heartily recommend politicians as sources.

As with any source, there is a tradeoff. If you expect to develop a politician as a long-term source, the tradeoff is that you will have to overlook signs of corruption in your source. You will lose a very valuable asset if you prove to be anything but 100% loyal to your politician-source. (If the corruption is really grave, it may be worth it to you to lose the asset. It's up to you.)

Rarely will an investigator develop a genuine friendship with a professional politician. Whatever relationship does develop will be called a "political friendship". To someone who hasn't been through it before, a political friendship will have all the signs of being genuine when in fact it is extremely temporary, is based only on mutual necessity, and is often unreliable. Don't let the trappings of friendship fool you or you'll be in for an emotional let-down.

You can also expect that your political friendship will be based on exchanging favors. Your political friend may help you with an investigation he or she has no personal interest in, but you, in turn, will be expected to help the politician.

In general, cultivating politicians as sources for a short-term investigation where there is mutuality of interest is a lot easier than cultivating a "political friendship".

The politician will be most likely to help you if he or she believes that you have some influence among people who may vote in an upcoming election. This is one source that the citizen investigator can access almost as easily as the full-time professional investigator or journalist. If you are investigating a subject that can possibly be of interest to a politician, by all means try to get that politician interested in your project. There are two types of things that will interest the politician -- investigations of problems in his or her legislative district that will make him or her look good to constituents if the problems are cleaned up; and special problems. Every politician has a special interest -- whether it's health care, welfare, minority rights, or national security. This interest extends beyond the politician's own legislative district. These are two distinct pools of excellent sources and you should make every effort to access them.

More specifically, let's say you are investigating problem "A".

If problem A has a geographic location, try to get help from politicians whose district includes that geographic location. Start with local politicians and work your way up to the House of Representatives and U.S. Senate. (You won't get much help from a Senator, but I suggest trying because if you're successful, the help you do get can be enormous.) Then look for those politicians who have a personal interest in problem A -- at all levels of government. In this pool you don't have to limit yourself to elected officials. Look around also for people in government agencies who are likely to be friendly to your approach and attitude.

For problem A, then, you'll have this potential pool of sources: city councilor or supervisor; county elected official; state representative, state senator; U.S. Representative; two U.S. Senators; and perhaps ten public officials who have an interest in problem A. If you try every potential source in that pool, you'll probably land yourself at least one good political source.

Take Harry's word for it: it's hard to beat a politician as a source.

CHAPTER 10
INFORMATION ANALYSIS

As your investigation progresses you will be accumulating a great deal of data from a variety of sources -- too much data to bother devoting mental energy to keeping track of. This chapter outlines a system of information management and analysis that I have successfully used for years to free my mental energy for more creative tasks. Each investigator develops his or her own information management and analysis system -- some are more effective than others, and their effectiveness depends largely on whether the system is suited to the personality of the user. So if my system doesn't work for you, don't use it. Create your own instead.

My system, which I call network analysis (other people call it "interlock analysis", or "common thread analysis"), may seem to require a lot of paperwork. It does, but don't let that dishearten you -- a 1979 survey of investigative journalists found that they spent about 30% of their time doing filing and other information-management related activities. The system I describe here can be easily tailored to computerization. In fact, at least two Congressional subcommittees have used this system with a computer for their investigations. These were the special Kennedy-King assassination committee, and a subcommittee studying ties between major U.S. corporations.

A good information management and analysis system should accomplish these things:

1) alert the analyst when data may be relevant to the investigation
2) enable selection of critical data from trivial data
3) make the status of information at hand clearly visible
4) assist the analyst in determining where investigative energies can be spent more effectively
5) make it possible to safely store and then retrieve original documentation as it is needed.

The time you spend maintaining a system that does the things described above will be more than made up for in the time you save in avoiding the "chicken-with-head-cut-off syndrome" -- running around in a hundred directions that aren't critical to your investigation.

File Organization

My investigations begin with two files: one with the name of my subject, and the other titled miscellaneous. These files house the documents I collect as my investigation progresses: notes, xerox copies of government filings, etc. At this stage -- generally the homework stage -- both files tend to get fat fairly fast. Soon it becomes obvious that I need more files. I create new files along two general categories: subject's key associates, and organizations that the subject deals with (this includes businesses). At this point I can usually remember what the relationship between each of these is, but I know this won't be true for long, so I begin the next phase of my system almost immediately.

Data Extraction

As I put materials into my files, I look at them and make notes about important data on separate index cards that can be alphabetized and cross-referenced. Deciding what data to extract is part intuition and part system. As a general rule these are the types of things I extract for my index-card collection:

1) The name of every key associate gets its own card on which is noted all of the information about the associate -- address, phone number, relationship to subject, the document that proves the relationship, dates of specific interactions with subject and what these interactions were, ties to organizations or companies with which the subject may be linked.

2) The name of every organization (or business) to which the subject is linked, if the organization seems important to the investigation. For example, if you were investigating a public official whom you think is getting kickbacks for influencing zoning decisions, any ties to construction companies, investment companies, etc., would tend to be important. It would not be important that the subject is a member of the Knights of Columbus.

3) Each officer of each organization to which the subject is linked, as determined in Step 2 above, is given a separate index card as well as being noted on the card for the organization. I generally include all of the officers including directors, advisors, president, vice-president, secretary, treasurer, legal agent, and anyone else who seems im-

Data Extraction, Example 1

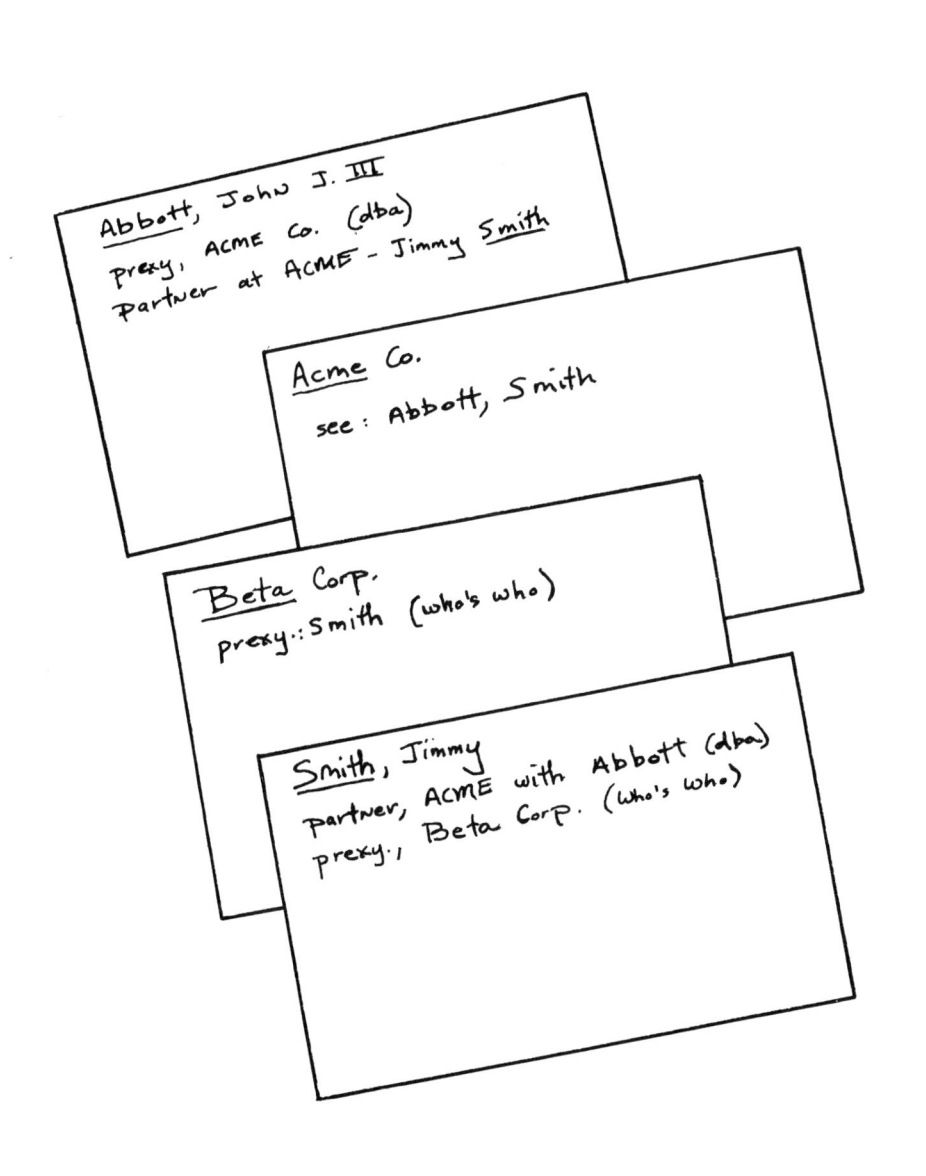

Abbott, John J. III
prexy, ACME Co. (dba)
partner at ACME - Jimmy Smith

Acme Co.
see: Abbott, Smith

Beta Corp.
prexy: Smith (who's who)

Smith, Jimmy
partner, ACME with Abbott (dba)
prexy, Beta Corp. (who's who)

Data Extraction, Example 2

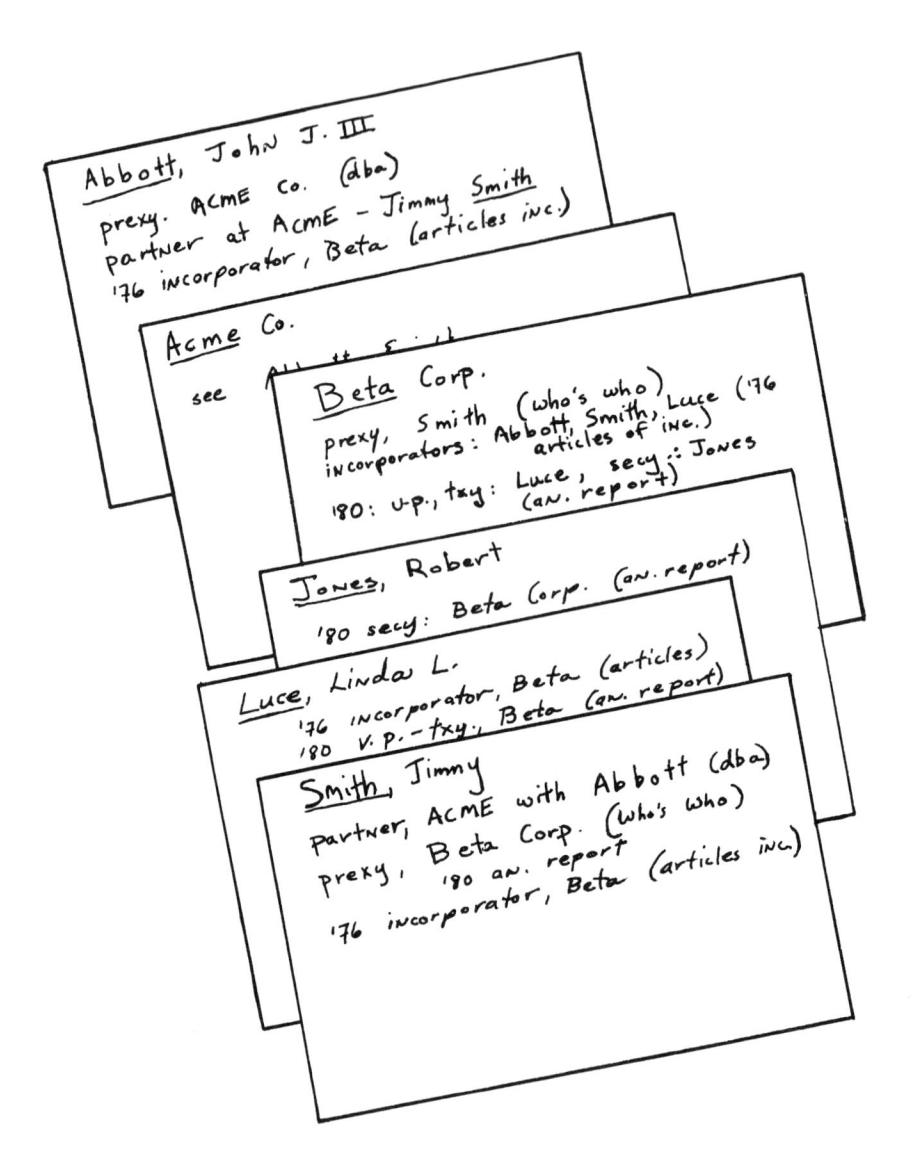

Abbott, John J. III
prexy, ACME Co. (dba)
partner at ACME - Jimmy Smith
'76 incorporator, Beta (articles inc.)

Acme Co.
see Abbott...

Beta Corp.
prexy, Smith (who's who)
incorporators: Abbott, Smith, Luce ('76 articles of inc.)
'80: v.p., txy: Luce, secy: Jones (an. report)

Jones, Robert
'80 secy: Beta Corp. (an. report)

Luce, Linda L.
'76 incorporator, Beta (articles)
'80 v.p.-txy, Beta (an. report)

Smith, Jimmy
partner, ACME with Abbott (dba)
prexy, Beta Corp. (who's who)
'80 an. report
'76 incorporator, Beta (articles inc.)

portant to the organization -- key staff people, etc.

At this point I generally find that ten original file folders of documents generate 100 or more index cards.

After a time, I begin to find that I am spending less time adding new index cards and more time adding information to index cards that already exist. That gives me the satisfying feeling that I'm getting somewhere in my investigation.

Here's an example. Let's say the subject, John J. Abbott, was president of Acme Co.. His partner at Acme, according to the dba filing, is Jimmy Smith. Jimmy Smith's *Who's Who* listing says that he is president of Beta Corp. The set of index cards would look like those in the example below (*Data Extraction, Example 1*).

The next documents I get are copies of Beta Corp.'s articles of incorporation and its latest annual filing. Bingo! I find that John J. Abbott was one of the original incorporators of Beta. I've uncovered a hidden connection or link between Abbott and Beta. If I'm lucky, later on down the road I'll find out that Beta is Acme's sole supplier, which will help to show that Abbott and Acme are violating local laws about competitive bidding on city contracts.

I update my index cards (as in *Data Extraction, Example 2*), open a new file on Beta Corp. and try to find out where I'm going to find documents to substantiate my theory that Beta is Acme's sole supplier.

At some point there will be too many data items for me to keep track of how they're related and which ones are important. Whenever I begin to feel lost in an investigation I progress to the next phase of my system.

Network Analysis

This phase involves drawing a chart that diagrams the important relationships between the subject, the subject's associates, and the organizations they are involved in. I like to use one symbol for people and a different one for organizations. Also, where it seems important -- especially where money changes hands -- I like to use a little arrow to show the flow of the money, goods, influence, or whatever.

Before going on to a real example of how I do network analysis, take a look at how I would draw the relationships between Abbott *et al.* in *Network, Abbott Example*, below.

Network, Abbott Example

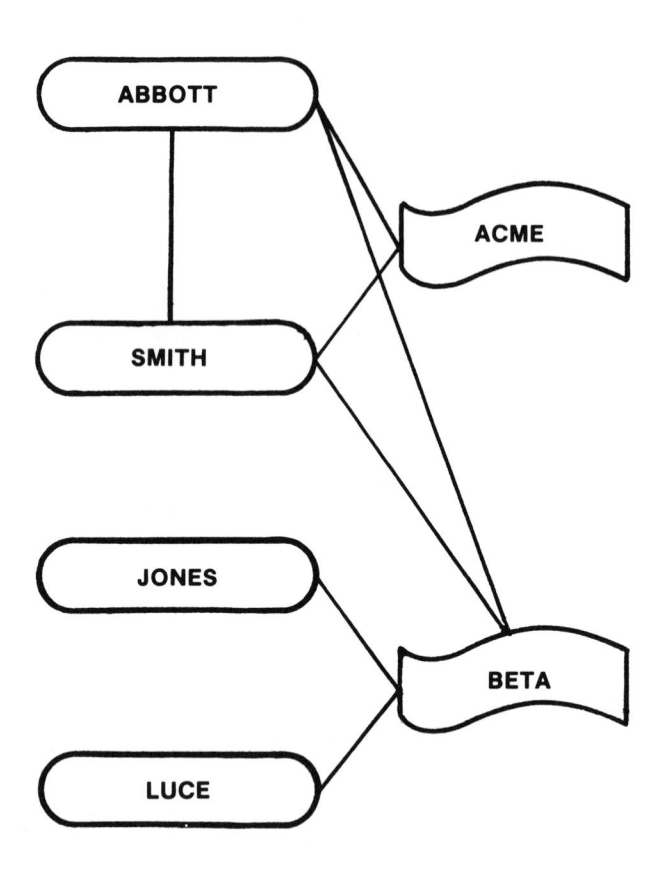

There is a line between Abbott and Smith because they are partners in Acme. There would also have been a line had they turned out to be brothers, or to have any other kind of somewhat personal relationship that extended beyond the purely functionary. Note that there are no lines between Jones & Luce because no relationship between them has been discovered yet.

(Another technique that I use on my network charts is to plot things I've heard but can't quite prove, in lines that are either a different color or are made out of dashes. Then when I prove the link I change the line.)

The *Abbott Network* diagrammed below shows me some possible avenues of exploration: are there ties between Acme and Beta; ties between Jones and the others; etc. As I come across such ties, "links", I add them to my chart.

And now, on to a real example of how I handle this type of analysis.

The example is Lyndon LaRouche, candidate for president in the 1980 Democratic primaries. (You may remember the excerpt from the LaRouche chronology earlier in this manual.) At this point the investigation is still pretty much in the homework stage and not all of that homework has been completed. However, so much data has been accumulated that it is beginning to get confusing. The purpose of this analysis, therefore, is to try to make some sense out of the data at hand and to discover what the next steps in the investigation should be.

Network Analysis: Lyndon LaRouche

This analysis will be done in two phases to keep the network charts "clean" and somewhat legible.

In this first phase I will examine some of the organizations LaRouche has been said to have control over or influence on. There are sixteen such businesses and organizations that have been operating in the last couple of years. However, at this point I only have data on ten of them.

One of the questions in a situation like this, where one person or a small group of people seem to control a large number of organizations, is whether they are violating any laws. There are several operant laws covering this collection of organizations, but this analysis is geared to three types of laws: federal elections law that prohibits corporations making donations to candidates for federal office; IRS law that strictly limits the involvement of tax exempt "charities" in politics; and a variety of laws that in general prohibit the formation of corporations for the purpose of fraudulently hiding financial assets in order to avoid having debts and court judgments collected. The U.S. Labor Party, one of the organizations in this maze, had lost a libel judgment of $35,000 and claimed that it had no assets with which to pay the judgment. In 1980, in fact, it no longer existed as an organization, according to spokespeople for LaRouche.

The set of data I will chart are:

Campaigner (Camp.), a magazine that in 1978 described itself as the theoretical journal of the U.S. Labor Party and the National Caucus of Labor Committees.

Campaigner Publications Inc. (CPI), according to postal permit information, publishers of *New Solidarity* and *Campaigner;* according to Federal Elections Commission filings, received money for its services from Citizens for LaRouche.

Citizens for LaRouche (CFL), Federal Elections Commission filings show it to be the principal campaign organization for Lyndon LaRouche's 1979-80 presidential bid. It purchased or ordered services from: CPI, New Solidarity International Press Service, and the National Caucus of Labor Committees.

Executive Intelligence Review (EIR). LaRouche campaign statements note that he has an "executive position" at this magazine. Its staff box notes that it is published by New Solidarity International Press Service.

Fusion (Fus.), monthly magazine of the tax-exempt Fusion Energy Foundation.

Fusion Energy Foundation (FEF), said, but not yet documented, to be founded by LaRouche.

New Solidarity (New S.), founded by LaRouche, according to his autobiography.

New Solidarity International Press Service (NSIPS), apparently has contractual relationship with *New Solidarity* as most news items in the publication carry the NSIPS dateline.

National Caucus of Labor Committees (NCLC), founded by LaRouche, according to autobiography and interviews.

U.S. Labor Party (USLP). LaRouche is apparently its chairman; it was founded as the political arm of the NCLC according to interviews. LaRouche ran on its presidential ticket in 1976.

LaRouche Network Chart #1

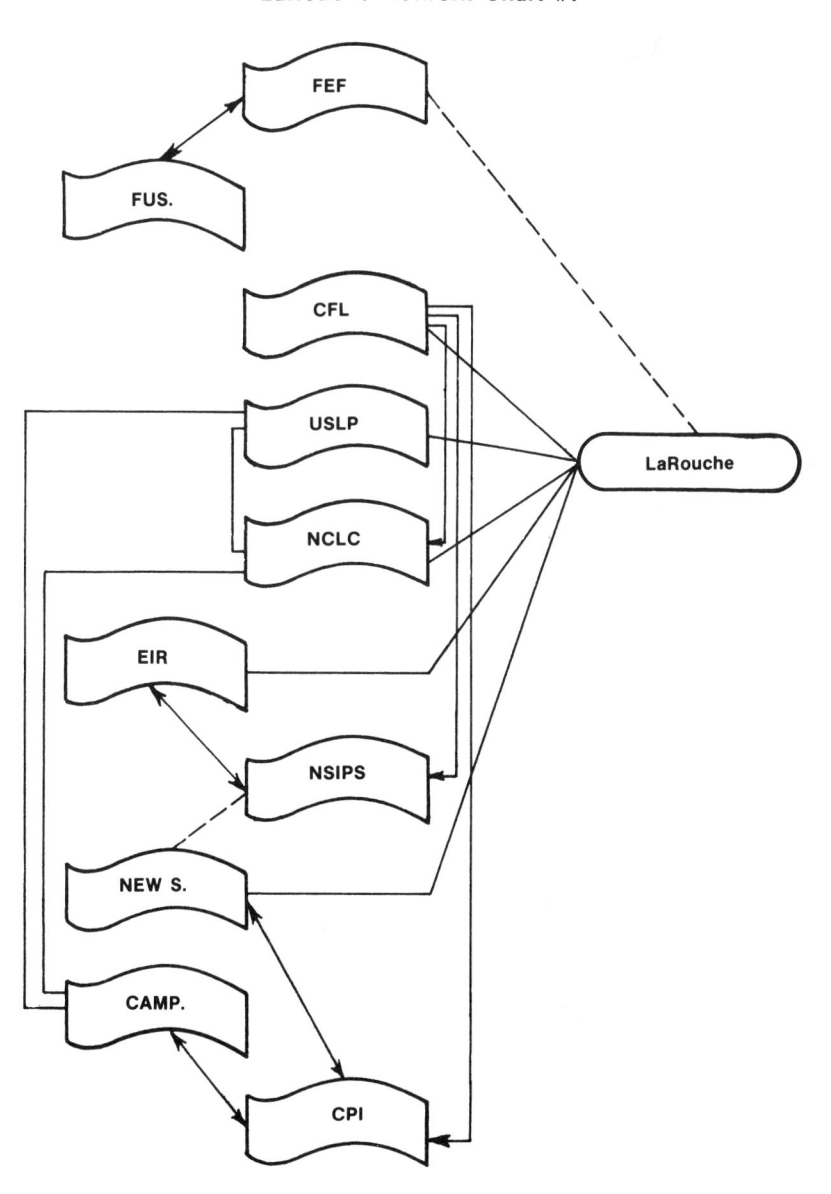

- FEF
- FUS.
- CFL
- USLP
- NCLC
- LaRouche
- EIR
- NSIPS
- NEW S.
- CAMP.
- CPI

105

The network chart (see *Chart 1*) maps out the relationships described above.

LaRouche Chart 2 will focus on key associates. Of 100 or so index-carded names of people who have links to one or more of the organizations charted, I have pulled out those people who have three or more direct or indirect ties. The data to be charted are:

Benton, Nick: '77-78, USLP candidate for governor of California, '79-80 California coordinator for CFL (interviews), '79-80 Southwest coordinator for FEF (*Fusion* magazine).

Dolbeare, Patricia: '76, NCLC executive committee (*Congressional Record*), '77-78, USLP candidate for superintendent of public instruction (flier), '79 northern California chair CFL (notes of public meeting).

Freeman, Debra (aka Debra Hanania): '78, USLP candidate for Congress, NCLC member, receives $2.5K/year from NSIPS (from deposition in libel suit); '79 contributed $250 to CFL (Federal Elections Commission).

Freeman, Lawrence ("Larry"): '76 NCLC executive committee (*Congressional Record*), chair Maryland USLP, receives $4K yearly from NSIPS (deposition), '79 contributed $250 to CFL. Related to Debra?

Freeman, Marsha: '79 NYC bureau EIR, energy news editor *Fusion*, *New Solidarity* column of science & technology (from publications). Related to Larry?

Hamerman, Nora: '76 NCLC exec. comm. (*Congressional Record*), '79 ed. board *Campaigner*, NYC bureau EIR, assoc. ed. *New Solidarity* (from publications).

Levitt, Morris: '76 NCLC exec. comm. (*Cong. Record*), '79 NYC bureau EIR, editor *Fusion,* official of FEF (publications).

Pepper, Dr. Stephen: '76 NCLC exec. comm. (*Cong. Record*), '79 co-owner Campaigner Publications (postal permit application), '79 CFL finance director (interview).

Spannaus, Nancy: '76 NCLC exec. comm. (*Cong. Record*), '78 ed. in chief USLP book DOPE, INC. (book); USLP trexy, management position at NSIPS (deposition); '79 cont. ed. EIR, '79 ed. board *Campaigner,* '79 ed. *New S.* (publications).

Steinberg, Jeffrey: '79 USLP chief of security (interviews), '79 NYC bureau NSIPS, '79 ed., counter-intelligence EIR (publications), paid money for services by CFL (Fed. elect. report).

LaRouche Network Chart #2

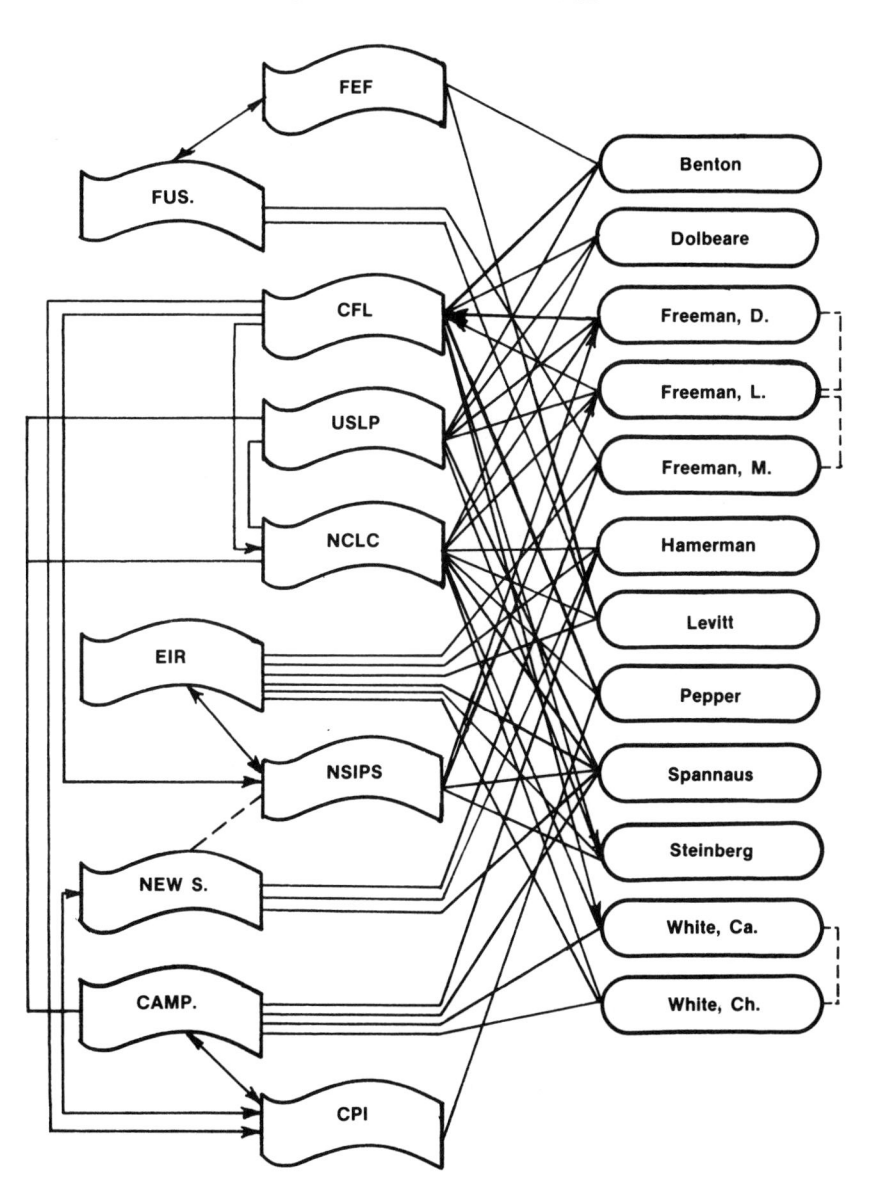

White, Carol (formerly Carol Schnitzer?): '76, NCLC exec. comm. (*Cong. Record*), '79 ed. in chief, *Campaigner* (publication), '79 CFL payment as political consultant (Fed. elect. report). Note: Schnitzer, who lived with LaRouche, was co-founder NCLC. Schnitzer left LaRouche. One source indicates she married Christopher White in England.

White, Christopher: '76 NCLC exec. comm. (*Cong. Record*), '79 contrib. ed. EIR, '79 ed. board *Campaigner* (publications). Related to Carol White?

(Note: CONGRESSIONAL RECORD is reference to: Extension of Remarks, Rep. Larry McDonald, Jan. 26, 1977, pp. E346-E348. Executive committee membership is said to be taken from NCLC publication.)

As before, known ties are indicated in a solid line, questionable ties are indicated in a broken line. Arrows indicate direction of flow of money. Additionally, some of the links between organizations are noted. If two organizations have direct ties, then it is possible that those people having ties to one organization might also have ties to the other organization. For example, Stephen Pepper, a co-owner of CPI, can be reasonably presumed to have some indirect ties to *Campaigner* and *New Solidarity*, two publications that are published by CPI. Those people with ties to *Campaigner* may have indirect ties to either USLP or NCLC because this publication was the "theoretical journal" of the two groups. Similarly, those with direct ties to NCLC may have indirect ties to the USLP because the USLP is the political arm of the NCLC.

What do the two network charts show?

- Of 12 people, 9 have direct links to NCLC, one may have an indirect link (Freeman, M.) if she is related to the other two Freemans, and two have links either to USLP or CFL.
- 7 of 12 have links to CFL
- Half have links to USLP
- Half have links to EIR
- 4 have links to NSIPS
- 4 have links to *Campaigner*
- Only 2 have links to FEF
- Of the NCLC-ers, five have ties to CFL and four have direct ties to the USLP while three more have indirect ties through *Campaigner.*

What does this data mean?

In my experience of doing such analyses I have seldom seen so many obvious interlocks between organizations. This suggests that pursuing them further might be worthwhile.

FEF appears to be the least likely to be in the direct control of the other organizations. This suggests that if there is a connection it is pretty carefully hidden or that in fact there is *no* connection that might violate IRS regulations.

If any organization is the "parent" of the others, it is doubtlessly NCLC, on whose executive committee most of the associates meet.

The relationship between CFL and the other organizations seems worth pursuing because of the high percentage of interlocks. This means I should check the rest of the CFL elections committee filings to see if there are other links. I am also curious if NSIPS is the Freemans' sole source of income. If it is, then it is possible to suggest that NSIPS is "laundering" money to CFL through payments to its staff. Such laundering is not in all cases against the law. It would be if NSIPS is a corporation, something that must be checked. It also would be if the total amount "laundered" were in excess of federal limits. Therefore, I'll have to find out what the legal organization is of NSIPS and try to determine who else is paid by them and if this is their sole source of income.

Other questions may occur to me as I re-examine the charts, but meanwhile I have come up with some direction for my investigation.

What has my system accomplished for me? It has allowed me to keep my original documentation in a safe place and to work from my index cards of extracted data. By the same token, the index cards refer me back to the documentation so that I can access it efficiently if I want to.

The data selection process has weeded out many data that aren't relevant to my investigation -- e.g., the names of all the people who had only one or two ties to the cluster of organizations.

The status of the data I have is visible on the network charts, on two sheets of paper that are easy to look at.

By analyzing the charts I have determined what I believe to be productive avenues for my investigation.

All of the criteria for a good data-management and analysis system have been met.

I can't think of much more to say about information analysis except one final hint: review the data you thought were trivial once in a while, and you may come up with something you missed at first.

CHAPTER 11
WHEN TO STOP AN INVESTIGATION

I doubt if any investigator really ever stops an investigation before finding out what he or she wanted to find out. Somehow, once you've asked a question, it won't rest until it has been answered.

But, at one point or another, it is sometimes necessary to stop an active investigation and put it on the back burner until you get a lucky break.

The most common reason for stopping an active investigation is running out of the money that is needed to continue it.

Other reasons for stopping active investigations include: not being able to complete an investigation before the statute of limitations on whatever crime is involved runs out; realizing that your subject is smarter than you are and that you will not be able to find the evidence you need to build a "case"; realizing that no one but you will give a damn what you find out about your subject; realizing that the "case" you're trying to build is phony.

In many of these situations a judgment could have been made early on in the investigation, or even before the investigation was begun, that it would not be a viable project. It saves a lot of time, energy and money if you can "stop" an investigation before you begin it.

Weighing The Decision

Before undertaking an investigation you should estimate the amount of energy and money it will take, if you are really the one to do it, and, how important the investigation is to you. Reject those investigations that don't satisfy *your* criteria -- there's plenty of dirt around and you'll soon find something more to your liking.

Most investigations seem to get started because someone approaches the investigator and says, "did you know that...?" "Did you know that's a CIA plot?" "Did you know that the mayor's on the take?" "Did you know...?" In short, most investigators begin with some kind of lead like this provided by a source. Some of the stories told by such walk-in sources would be great, if they were true. Unfortunately, about nine in ten are sheer rumor or speculation and have no ground in fact.

Sometimes it is hard to know which of the ten leads is valid and which of them are dead-ends. By using your judgment and a couple of tests on your walk-in source, you may be able to eliminate five of the dead-end leads in every batch of ten.

The key to evaluating leads is familiarity with the general subject area. If you have had, let's say, a lot of experience in investigations involving the CIA, you'll be able to judge what falls into the Company pattern and what doesn't and thereby eliminate a lot of spurious leads. Same goes for any other subject area. I encourage you to develop a background in many areas of investigation -- it makes for variety and helps you be prepared for anything. But if a lead comes to you out of the blue and deals with an area you're not familiar with, before following it down a rosy path, check it out with friends and contacts who *do* have experience in that subject area. (I'll never forget the hours I spent trying to prove a conspiracy between the John Birch Society and the Klan. It was foreign territory to me and I wasted a lot of time on that dead-end. Needless to say, had I asked a few people with some familiarity with both clusters of organizations I would have never have begun the investigation.)

Aside from familiarity with the subject, you should try to test every walk-in source to determine their credibility. Always ask the source how he or she knows that what he/she is saying is true. Then ask if he or she can prove it. These two questions will both allow the source to come up with any documentation the source may have, and will allow you to see if the source knows what he/she is talking about. Additionally, it will help you a great deal if you do undertake the investigation, if your first source is around to help point you to other sources and leads. If your source disappears after dropping the story in your lap, you're in for a lot of work should you decide to undertake an investigation.

After you've weeded out the leads into the category of 20% chance that it is a genuine lead, then you should weigh your own capabilities and interests against the information before accepting an investigation. Here are a few questions you should ask yourself:

• Do you have a pool of contacts in the subject area who can help you or do you have to start at the beginning?

• What area of the law applies to this investigation -- is it an

area that is difficult to prove, like murder, or a simple white collar crime that has an easy-to-follow paper trail?
- Is the material you'll need to complete the investigation available to you locally or will you have to spend a lot of money in other cities and states tracking it down?
- And, most important -- does the investigation arouse your passionate interest? If you aren't passionately interested in the subject, you'll be spending a lot of time wishing you'd never begun the investigation -- hand the lead over to a friend who *does* care about it.

Two Traps

There are two deadly traps awaiting any good investigator. The first trap is *the personal vendetta*. The second is *the conspiracy trap*.

If you're competent, you know that you have the capability of getting revenge against your personal enemies. Often it is very tempting. The only difficulty is that you may be the only person in the world who gives a damn about the case you can build against Joe or Josephine Smith. This may sound like moralizing, but actually it's quite pragmatic -- put this type of investigation on the back burner. If your enemy is as bad as you think, the person will eventually hang him or herself. Lay back and be ready to pounce when your enemy has done him or herself in. Why waste your time and energy doing something your enemy will eventually do for you?

The second trap is really a great deal more dangerous than the first. In the vendetta investigation all you waste is your time and money. The conspiracy investigation can drive you to the nuthouse. This warning about conspiracies has absolutely nothing to do with whether they exist or don't exist. Doubtlessly, conspiracies occur all the time. Remember the discussion of friendship networks in the section on developing "inside" sources? Remember the finding that an average of only five people separates anyone from anyone else? This fact works to your advantage when you're looking for sources. It works to your disadvantage when you're trying to follow a conspiracy.

Take this hypothetical example from the JFK assassination. Among the names that came up in connection with Oswald and Jack Ruby was David Ferrie of New Orleans. When the assassination was still being investigated by the Warren

Commission one of my friends mentioned to me that one of my sources had known Ferrie. It sounded like a great lead to the story of the century. The trouble was that the source who knew Ferrie was not only keeping his mouth shut about it, but was also a police informer. Wow -- maybe this pointed to some kind of conspiracy in a police agency. In an investigation like this, the normal technique is to trace current associates of the subject (in this case the guy who knew Ferrie) in order to come up with one or more who go back in time to the date the events occurred. In this case I was hoping to find co-conspirators, which meant that all of the subject's associates were suspect. The trap shut when I began doing network charts: *everyone* had a link to someone who had a link to the subject (who had a link to Ferrie who in turn allegedly had a link to the assassination). It became a very small world indeed as I grew suspicious of virtually everyone from Rockefeller down to some of my co-workers. In other words, I had entered that mental state known as paranoia. Plots within plots were surfacing all around me and I began to feel that I was being followed, that my phones were being tapped, that my life was in some danger. (Actually, I later discovered, my phone *had* been tapped, but for another reason entirely.)

Fortunately, I bailed out of the investigation before I became a certifiable paranoid. Other investigators have not been so lucky. They have followed the conspiracy trail into paranoia and literally into the nuthouse. Maybe they were right about their conspiracy theories and maybe their paranoia was justified. The tragedy of it was simply that they ended up being very unhappy people.

That's the deadly trap of conspiracy investigations -- one lead takes you to another until most of the world is somehow linked to the conspiracy. It's a frightening place and I would urge you to stay away from it.

The Value Of Waiting

As I said at the beginning of this chapter, no investigator ever really drops an investigation -- many simply end up on the back burner with the investigator waiting for a lucky break. Amazingly, those lucky breaks *do* come along.

Sometimes your subject's desperation will cause him or her to blow it. If you've done your homework on your subject, then you'll be in a position to take advantage of your subject's tactical errors very quickly.

Here's an example of creative waiting. It's not very dramatic, but it demonstrates the point. Several years ago I closed an investigation on a direct mail specialist who was well known for his political fund-raising. His name was Richard Viguerie, who some people liked to call the "Godfather of the New Right". By the time I had closed my investigation, the Godfather was already losing some of his grip as a political king-maker. Apparently, as time went by, he got into a financial crunch and became a bit desperate for money. Among the "don'ts" in New Right politics is involvement with organizations that are publicly known as anti-Jewish. Associations like those are bad business for New Right king-makers. About four years after I'd closed the investigation, someone sent me a direct mail piece for an organization called Liberty Lobby which has been targeted by the Jewish Anti-Defamation League as one of the most influential anti-Jewish organizations in the country. It's funny, but after a long investigation, certain key data seem never to leave your memory. I noticed that the postal permit for the Liberty Lobby mailing was "No. 57, Waldorff, Maryland". I remembered that number quite clearly. It was the number used by a corporation owned by Viguerie. It took me about ten minutes to dig the documentation out of my files, call the corporation to make sure I wasn't seeing things, and I had my story. As it turned out, once the story got around, the Godfather's reputation became a bit more tarnished.

At other times creative waiting involves waiting for new leads and sources to turn up. Here's one investigation that I am still waiting for a lucky break on. Maybe you can help.

In the mid-70s an anonymous document was circulated in far right political circles that accused a lot of people of, among other things, being homosexuals. It was an intriguing bit of black propaganda. The document, which came to be known as the "DeGuello" manuscript, had been mailed (no return address) to key leaders in the far right. (I later estimated the total number of people who got original copies to be about 100). "DeGuello" caused quite a stir and hundreds of copies were xeroxed and passed around. There were enough facts in "DeGuello" to make some of the accusations sound convincing, and just about every right wing leader was accused of something. The effects of "DeGuello" were to foment distrust in the right with the obvious intent of disrupting its effectiveness. For about one or two years "DeGuello" succeeded in achieving this goal.

The puzzle about "DeGuello" was: Who was the author?

The anonymous author claimed to be a group of patriotic people with ties to government security services.

Whoever it was knew a whole lot about the right wing -- not only the names and addresses of 100 or more leaders, but a *lot* of facts about their lives.

It was the best example of black propaganda I've ever seen, and I'd love to meet the authors. Lots of speculations were made about the authors. Some people blamed the FBI, others blamed the U.S. Labor Party, and others blamed three different right-wing leaders. Others blamed foreign intelligence operations. I spent a good three months trying to track down the mysterious authors of "DeGuello" and never came up with any hard evidence pointing to anyone.

As I said, the investigation is still on the back burner and I'm creatively waiting for a stroke of luck to provide me with *the* lead to the authors. I hope you can help me. Meanwhile, it's the only investigation that I haven't satisfactorily closed. But one of these days I'll find the lead I need. I have faith. So should you.

Harry's Seventeenth Law: **Never give up hope.**

CHAPTER 12
PROTECTING SOURCES

Toward the end of the 1970s, investigators who worked for newspapers and magazines began to find that they faced going to jail for refusing to give courts information about their investigations and their confidential sources. As with every controversy, there were two sides to the issue: newspapers argued that they had been given extra rights under the First Amendment to the Constitution; courts argued that newspapers had no more First Amendment rights than any other citizens. As the 1980s began, newspapers, magazines, and television stations were preparing a fight to the death to protect confidential sources and information. Several trade journals began making the claim that investigative journalists were going to have to develop FBI-like techniques just to get their work done.

Protecting sources and confidential information involves much more than refusing to disclose information. Laws are now adequate for police and other investigators to track down a person's sources: newspaper files are no longer protected from searches; and just about anyone who wants to can get hold of a copy of the telephone numbers you have called.

Again, this is not a moral issue. You can choose to reveal your sources or choose not to reveal them. The suggestions listed below to protect sources and information can be used or ignored. They are given so that you, the investigator, can control the decision of whether or not to reveal sources and information.

The investigator is in a double-bind because he or she must retain documents and evidence in case of a libel or defamation of character suit. Meanwhile, those very documents contain the clues that will reveal confidential sources.

Document Protection

The problem is to have access to your documents and evidence when you need it, and not to know where it is when someone else is looking for it.

The rules of document protection are somewhat simple:

1) Make three copies of your documents. Keep one set where you can get hold of it easily when you need to use it (remember, most often you'll be using the data you've extracted from the documents and not the documents themselves) or destroy it. Destroy your set *before* a court orders you to produce it. The second set should go to an attorney you really trust where it will probably be protected by attorney-client privilege. (Watch for changes in this law -- the government is working overtime to break through the attorney-client privilege barrier.) The third set should go to a trusted friend who should secure them without telling you where the documents are secured. Your friend, in this case, is your last line of defense. Assuming that you've destroyed your copy of the document package, that the attorney ploy has fallen through, and that you are asked where any other copies are stored, you can honestly, and without perjury, say that you don't know. Theoretically, if your friend's security is in danger of being jeopardized, the documents can be passed along with the same instructions you gave to your friend.

2) When you create documents, for example notes of an interview with a source you wish to protect, make sure that your documents do not contain information you wouldn't want published. This maneuver can be handled by giving your sources code names and creating a key to those names (which includes their real names, addresses and phone numbers) which you secure in a different location from your documents.

3) Stay in touch with laws regarding libel, invasion of privacy, and defamation of character. Your primary reason for needing a set of evidence is to protect yourself in the event you are sued for libel or other related "crimes". Like most laws, these laws also have a statute of limitations. At this writing, whoever believes they have been victimized by something you have printed has one year from the date they became aware of the material to sue you. I suggest that you take advantage of a very common practice among journalists, and that is sending complementary copies of your story to your subject. Then, using a pretext, get your subject to admit to having seen the story. After that is done, you only have to sweat things out for one year. After the year is up, if you feel like it, simply destroy all three sets of your document package. (Before destroying your evidence, be sure to get advice from a lawyer specializing in libel and related laws. The time period in which a victim can bring suit may be changed, or it may vary under special circumstances.)

Source Protection

Again, the investigator is placed in a double-bind, but this one is somewhat easier to manage. Theoretically, before you publish the results of your investigation, you will have thoroughly checked out your source to make sure he or she is reliable. After so much checking out, one would think it would be a simple matter to tell the court the name and location of your source. Here are some ground rules that may help you maintain the security of your sources:

1) When you interview a source who demands protection, make sure that the source does not tell you about any crimes etc. that he or she may have participated in that do not *directly* relate to your investigation. Prevent your source from any needless self-incrimination. For example, all your source has to do is tell you he or she saw someone do something -- the source does not have to admit he or she participated in it.

2) When working with a source who demands protection, the question of getting an affidavit to protect yourself can be a nagging one. The affidavit could eventually blow your source. The ideal situation is to take a witness with you to the interview. Your witness can take the place of an affidavit if necessary. There is no particular reason why your witness need even know the source's name -- the time, date, place of the interview, and what was said are all that is really important.

3) If you need to call your source on the phone, do so from a phone booth (and *not* the booth next door to your house or office).

4) If your source has documents that you need, arrange to have the source mail them to you in an envelope without a return address. If you're asked, you can always honestly say that you don't really know where the documents came from -- you got them in an unmarked envelope. (This is called *maintaining deniability.*)

5) If possible, use your source not as a primary witness to an illegal act, but for background only. Try to locate other sources to confirm the story so that you don't have to use the source you are protecting.

6) Depending on your situation, you might give this strategy some thought: you can't reveal your source if you can't be found.

7) I've been lucky with source protection. I have a wonderfully trained memory. It is very selective. After I have checked a source's bonafides, gotten the data down with a witness, I no longer remember the name of the source, how I met the source, or any other information about the source. This isn't a jest or a ruse. I have, in fact, taken lie-detector tests and found that I really can't remember some things...

General Security

Investigators who are new to the scene often make the mistake of bragging about how they got their information. I guess it makes them feel important. Eventually, however, word gets out, and the investigator's contacts dry up. Bragging is self-defeating.

Train yourself to observe the "need to know" rule. Don't tell anyone anything that you don't have to tell them. Take your pleasure from seeing the subjects of your investigations get the punishment they deserve, not from blabbing about how you did it.

CHAPTER 13
CAN YOU PROVE IT?

At last, you have reached the time when you're ready to report the results of your investigation, either because you're ready to close the investigation or because you've uncovered material that must be reported as soon as possible.

One more step lies before you -- checking your facts. It is your last chance to make sure your investigation is built on a solid foundation before risking your reputation on your report. It's time to play devil's advocate with your work. It's time to measure your work against *Harry's Eighteenth Law:* **Never report anything unless you can prove it.**

Harry's 18th is no more moralistic than any other of the laws. It is based on pragmatic self-interest. Again, whatever benefit accrues to the public comes only as a byproduct of the investigator insuring his or her self-interest. At stake here is your reputation, and your good name is what makes your information a marketable commodity.

If something in your report can't be substantiated, you can be sure that *someone* will notice it. And if a careful reader finds one questionable item, he or she will wonder how many others are also wrong. Depending on the importance of the datum that is in error, your own credibility as an investigator may also be called into question.

For example, *Public Eye*, a left-oriented magazine, had, through careful reporting of its investigations, developed a fairly high credibility rating despite its obvious slant. Then in 1979 the publication apparently underwent some changes. What gave the show away was an article that charged that the World Anti-Communist League, the CIA, and a "division of Spanish mercenaries" were responsible for a terrorist attack on Rome's DaVinci airport in 1973 that left 32 people dead. The 1973 attack, however, had been carried out by the Palestine Liberation Organization (PLO). Those readers who were aware of PLO involvement in the attack not only lost faith in the particular article, which claimed to expose the World Anti-Communist League, but in the publication as a whole.

The guidelines outlined in this chapter are designed to help eliminate such errors in your reports. Many journalists may regard the guidelines as much more stringent than those they are used to. They are, however, guidelines that are generally followed by top-notch public investigators. If you follow them, your error-rate will be reduced to nearly zero, and you'll build a solid reputation for credibility.

How Many Sources?

Your sources may be classified into two types: primary and secondary. Primary sources include: documents signed or published by your subject or his/her agents, public records like property titles and court judgments, and those things you have seen or heard for yourself if you have documented your observations carefully and in a timely manner. Secondary sources include everything and everyone else.

In general, if you are using a primary source, then you do not need to get confirmation from another source although it is a good idea, where possible, to have a witness to the things you have seen or heard.

If you use a secondary source, you should have it confirmed by another, independent, secondary source, or by a primary source. Additionally, you should have good reason to believe that your secondary sources are reliable. In other words, if Father Smith says he saw your subject steal something, you should try to locate someone else who also saw the theft. Secondary sources include some documents that are internal to an organization or the private property of your subject -- accounting records, for example. You must have good reason to believe that the records are what you think they are and aren't forgeries. Try to get the accountant who completed them to identify them as being what you think they are.

As you can probably guess, it's a lot safer and easier to work with primary sources only.

Unfortunately, not all subjects incriminate themselves in primary documents or while you are watching. So secondary sources are invaluable and necessary to almost every investigation. Most investigations are based on a combination of primary and secondary data. Getting at least two secondary sources to confirm an item of information is sometimes a lot more trouble than you think it's worth. But if you're skeptical of your subject's activities, then you should apply your skepticism evenly. Father Smith, after all, may have some reason for lying.

Or, being more generous, Father Smith may not have seen what he thought he saw.

An ideal world would have all its crooks incriminating themselves either in primary documents or in front of at least wo independent and reliable witnesses. Some crooks do. Most do not and that's why investigators are often left with, at best, only one secondary source who can testify to a criminal act. In fact, the investigator is lucky if he or she can find even this much evidence. If the rules on sources described above were to be strictly followed, a great many investigations would never be closed. So, as with most rules, the rules on sources have their exceptions.

If you have only a secondary source to back up your "case" against your subject you should realize that your *own* credibility is going to be tied to your source's credibility. That should make you think long and hard before using a single unsupported secondary source.

Here are a few guidelines for using unsupported secondary sources:

1) You should have reason to believe that the source is reliable and go to some lengths to prove that the source is not lying to you or is not misinterpreting things.

2) What the source tells you should fit logically into the pattern of evidence you have developed from other sources.

3) Your source will have to be willing to comment for attribution.

4) When you make your report you must quote this source directly and not paraphrase.

5) Before making your report you must give your subject a chance to explain or respond to the charges made by your source (if you're lucky, your subject will incriminate him/herself at this time).

6) When you make your report you must include what your subject said in response to the charges.

In my experience, the sources that I've been unable to get confirmation for have usually been pretty unreliable types who talk because they're out to get revenge or who are so doped up one would wonder if everything they see isn't actually an hallucination. They're often crooks themselves.

Another reason I'm afraid of single secondary sources is

because there are so many pathological liars running around. Pathological liars can fool lie detector machines -- and me as well.

So, as far as I am personally concerned, I usually don't want to be bothered with these types of sources. I'll listen to them and if their story is important enough, I'll spend a little time trying to get confirmation, but I know that I'm usually running down a blind alley. Also, I'm pretty lazy. If I have only one witness to a murder and that witness isn't very reliable and I don't have any other evidence to support that case, I'd much rather go after some dirt that I *can* prove. A murder case built on only a single unreliable witness will be laughed right out of the DA's office. A good IRS fraud case, however, might net the subject a stint in prison. It's a lot easier on me that way and the results are more satisfying.

Common Mistakes

One of the most common mistakes investigators tend to make, including myself, is not leaving room in the report for "deniability". In other words, instead of simply recounting the evidence I've accumulated, I'll tend to jump to the conclusion that the evidence proves something illegal or unfavorable. This can leave an investigator caught in a really tight corner called *libel*.

In order to leave myself room to maneuver and to deny that some error in my reports was my *own* creation, before handing in a final report, I'll go back through what I've put down and add in a good measure of two wonderful word-tools: "according to", and "apparently".

Here are a few sample sentences to give you a feel for what I mean. They are followed by a revised and "deniable" version:

- Schwartz did not report his gambling winnings.
- Schwartz *apparently* did not report...
- Carto died in the accident. It was the first time he had driven his new car.
- *...According to* his mother, it was the first time he had driven...
- The gang is the largest in St. Louis.
- *According to* police, the gang is the largest...
- These actions are in violation of state statute.
- The *evidence indicates* violations of state statutes. OR

- These actions, *according to* the state attorney, violate...OR
- These actions *apparently* violate state statutes.

Even when material isn't libelous, it's always a good idea to be on the safe side and to add a qualifier that makes what you say "deniable". Take the St. Louis gang from the example above. Everyone in town might know that the gang is the largest. But I'll bet you that if you report that it is, someone will come along and show you evidence that you are wrong. That's just the way things are.

A second mistake that is very common is the implication of guilt by association. (The network-analysis system described in Chapter 10 of this manual is especially vulnerable to this kind of error, so it must be used carefully.) The fact that someone is a member of an organization, an employee of a company, a supplier to a company or organization, is written about by an organization's publication, or is a relative of your subject does not *necessarily* mean that he or she is aware of or would approve of what your subject is doing. It's alright to let the reader come to a conclusion about guilt based on an association that you mention, but don't make such a conclusion yourself unless you have substantiated it. Additionally, most officers of corporations and organizations are often legally responsible for what the group does, whether they know about it, approve, or disapprove. So don't become overly paranoid about publishing people's associations with questionable activities and individuals. Just remember that you may be way off base in your assessment. That Klan leader, for example, just might be an infiltrator from a communist organization or from the Bureau of Alcohol, Tobacco, and Firearms.

Fact Checking

I have yet to meet anyone who enjoys this element of the investigation process, so I doubt that you'll like it either. However, there are two saving graces about fact checking. First, and most important, giving your report a final check will save you from making embarrassing errors, and second, it gets easier each time you do it.

Once you have prepared your report, make a copy of it. Number the lines of each page to make things easier on yourself later. Then, go through each line carefully and underline or circle *every* fact you have written. This includes names, dates, places, numbers, amounts of money, specific actions you describe, quotes... everything.

Next, pretend you're being sued for libel and your entire financial future depends on proving each of the statements you've underlined. Meanwhile, get your original files out.

Then, for every statement you have underlined, locate the documents that support it.

Beginning with the first statement you've underlined, label the supporting documents "Exhibit A", and, on a separate page, keep a list of the documentation for each statement. This list will be the index to your documentation package.

(The sample work in the appendix EDITING FOR ACCURACY should help you.)

As you go through your report this way, you'll find that some statements require only one document, while others require several. For example, if you're reporting on five corporations and you say that J. Edwards is president of all five, you'll need copies of the articles of incorporation or annual reports for each of the five. You should keep to one major identifier per statement, for example "A", and append a subscript for each document in the set: e.g., A-1, A-2, A-3, etc.

As you follow this procedure, you'll probably find at least one statement that you somehow knew you could document, but now cannot. Mark these statements with a big "X" -- you'll either have to find the proof or drop them from your report; meanwhile, you may turn up the document you thought you had as you go through the rest of the material.

More often, you'll catch yourself in simple mistakes. Sometimes you'll find that your documents don't say exactly what you thought (or hoped) they did. Whatever the case, if you've made an error, correct it to show what your documents actually say.

Don't be overwhelmed if the documents pile up -- I recently finished a 5,000 word report (about 20 pages) and the documentation package had 48 major exhibits (necessitating a second run through the alphabet, beginning AA). The total number of pages in the documentation package was 176 -- and some of those individual documents substantiated several statements.

# # #

When you've reached the last word of the last sentence and

gone back and taken care of all the spots checked off with an "X", you're done. Your investigation is closed. You've done a good solid job of work and it's probably a lot better than most of the stuff that passes for investigative journalism today.

Congratulations!

CHAPTER 14
DO IT ELECTRONICALLY

The best news for the citizen investigator since the first edition of this book was published has been the take-off of the home-computer revolution. Not only can your computer play games and take over your filing and cross-referencing chores, a home computer lets you plug into a new world of electronically stored data.

Until recently, computerized data bases have been available only to the government or to academic and economic elites who had access to computers costing hundreds of thousands of dollars. Today anyone with $100 can buy a computer, can connect it to a $100 modem, plug it into the phone jack and tap into the network world. Data is no longer a commodity available to a racial, class or gender elite. Just connect your computer to a modem, plug into the wall jack and the world is open to you.

Want to research someone's *Who's Who* listings for the past few years? Let your computer call *BRS* or *DIALOG*. Want to know the nitty gritty about a publicly-held corporation? Call up Dow Jones Information and Retrieval Service.

There are more than 100 public electronic data bases. These contain data that can be retrieved in seconds over the telephone — a tremendous time and money saver for citizen investigators who have limited research budgets. Now you can live two hundred miles from the nearest airport and access a company's complete Securities and Exchange Commission filings just as easily as can the Manhattan native. In fact, the Manhattan native is probably using a computer at his or her home or office to spare the expense and hassle of a trip to the SEC.

Here's a sample of what you can find on unrestricted public data bases (aside from dozens of directories and *Who's Whos*):

Auto-Cite: 3,500,000 records of opinions in federal court cases.

Lexis: 1,250,000 records on legal and legislative affairs — a good source for information from individual states.

Foundation Directory: 4,000 records — includes most recent IRS 990 filings for nonprofit corporations with assets of $1,000,000 or more.

National Newspaper Index: complete indexes of the *New York Times*, the *Wall Street Journal*, and the *Christian Science Monitor*.

NDEX: more than 1,000,000 citations; an index of news from the *Chicago Sun Times*, the *Chicago Tribune*, the *Denver Post*, the *Detroit News*, the *Houston Post*, the *Los Angeles Times*, the *New Orleans Times Picayune*, the *San Francisco Chronicle*, the *Washington Post*, and the *St. Louis Post Dispatch*. Entries date back to 1976.

And, from restricted, but still public, data bases:

Dun & Bradstreet Inc.'s data base includes complete reports on more than four million U.S. companies, including data on the companies' top management.

TRW's Credit Data Service is the largest public data base in the U.S. It has records on eighty million of us. That's even larger than the files of major credit card companies (VISA, the largest, has only sixty-five million accounts).

Private data bases (the government's, for example), are much more difficult to access than public ones. But if you're tempted, you're much more likely to succeed in an illegal computer break-in than you are in person. The movie *War Games* is not so far removed from reality as the government would like us to think. (In fact, getting access to Department of Defense computers is fairly easy.)

There are some drawbacks to electronic research.

The first drawback is that data bases contain only that — data. What you need is information. Information is the meaning that you derive from data. It's very compelling when you're sitting down in front of an automatic data-retrieving machine to get all the data you can. In fact, data collecting can be addictive. Data that has no information value to you will only confuse the important issues of your reports. So once you're plugged in, remember what you're there for and don't get distracted by the siren calls of the data you can't use.

Harry's First Electronic Law: **Data are not information.**

Related to this law is the unfortunate fact that you may only find 10 to 20 percent of the data you need for your information profile with your trusty computer and speedy modem. Old fashioned legwork is still the name of the game. But anything that makes your life easier is worth the investment.

The second, and probably the greatest drawback to electronic research is that it will take you a good deal of time to learn how to search a data base properly so that you get all the data you are looking for with as little fat as possible. The biggest hurdle here seems to be people's reluctance to understand that computers can't read. All computers can do is sense electronic impulses and compare them to other electronic impulses. A computer ascribes no meaning to your words. If you tell the machine to search for "theft," for example, you will get references to every citation that includes the word "theft." But you'll miss citations that use words like "robbery" instead of "theft." So remember *Harry's Second Electronic Law:* **Computers can't read.**

Fortunately, many of the largest data-base vendors (a vendor is someone who sells access to other people's data bases) supply good information on how to design a good search. You can get some of the best information on how to do an efficient search from Dialog, the largest data base vendor in the U.S. Dialog also offers free classes in how to use the 200 data bases they offer. Write to: Dialog, 3460 Hillview Ave., Palo Alto, CA 94304, for free information. I use Dialog very often because they have a big selection of data bases, I pay only for what I use, and I can order a copy of the original document I've studied electronically. This last feature is very handy because many of the references on the data bases aren't available through my local library.

In addition to its regular service, Dialog offers a discount evening service called *Knowledge Index* which is a good place to begin to learn about data bases and search strategies. The service costs only $12.00 for each hour you use and there are no hidden charges.

The third drawback to computer searching can be cost. Some vendors charge you a sign-up fee just to get a password. This fee can be as much as $1000 per year. Some specialized data bases have prohibitive hourly charges — up to $400 an hour for some legal data bases, for example. Many vendors also charge a minimum monthly fee whether you use the service or data base or not. In addition, some vendors charge you a fee for the computer storage space in which they store your account information. Watch out for these hidden costs.

Harry's Third Electronic Law: **Always be friendly to librarians and information brokers.**

Some librarians may subscribe to the data base services you need and trained librarians can provide an inexpensive way for you to access very expensive data bases.

Another source of help, especially if your local library is not set up to operate in the network world, is a free-lance information broker. An information broker is someone who sells data and documentation that has been retrieved either manually or electronically from public (and sometimes private) data bases. The broker carries service sign-up fees as overhead so the cost is spread between many clients. Also, the broker is an expert at finding data fast and will use far less computer time than you would use. So although the broker, who will charge $25 to $75 per hour in addition to data base hourly access rates, may seem expensive, you may be getting a real bargain.

You may also get some good ideas on how to pursue your investigation further from either your librarian or your information broker. Don't overlook these two good sources in the electronic world.

Good luck using electronic data bases to speed up your work and make it more interesting. Some of the materials in Appendix 3 may be a good place for you to begin if you're not already plugged in to the world connection!

APPENDIX 1
HARRY'S LAWS

1. There is dirt on everyone.
2. Anyone can dig up the dirt on anyone else if they want to badly enough.
3. If Harry can do it, anyone can.
4. Go for the jugular.
5. There's nothing like a good felony rap to really cut your subject's jugular.
6. Know the law.
7. Think like a crook.
8. Get all the public records you can.
9. The more you learn about your subject, the easier it is to learn more.
10. Get your friends to help you.
11. Look for your subject's enemies.
12. Always be friendly to accountants and secretaries.
13. Document everything you can.
14. Make things easy on yourself by making things easy for your sources.
15. Before beginning an interview, be thoroughly prepared.
16. Never take any risk you can avoid.
17. Never give up hope.
18. Never report anything unless you can prove it.

HARRY'S ELECTRONIC LAWS

1. Data are not information.
2. Computers can't read.
3. Always be friendly to librarians and information brokers.

APPENDIX 2
EDITING FOR ACCURACY

The following sequence of materials includes:
1. A rough draft report prepared for fact-checking.
2. The same rough draft report after the available documentation has been found and itemized.
3. A sample index of documentation.
4. An edited report that corrects for mistakes and sloppiness in the rough draft.
5. An analysis of the edited report to show what the changes accomplished and why they were made.

Rough Draft Report*

1 At least three campaign irregularities have been traced
2 to the organization in California.
3   The first campaign was a mayoral race. The candidate's
4 committee filed false reports of expenditures with both
5 city and state governments.
6   The second campaign was the mayoral run-off election
7 a month later. The organization sponsored an effort to
8 oppose the incumbant mayor. In its own journal, the group
9 said that 50,000 fliers had been distributed in this
10 effort. No report, however, was filed with either city
11 or state officials as was required by law.
12   The third campaign law violation occurred in the
13 presidential race. Although the organization made expenditures
14 in the state on behalf of the candidate, it failed to
15 report them to the Secretary of State as is required by
16 Federal Elections law.

--30--

*As this version is not correct, I have deleted the name of the organization from the rough draft report. It appears in the final report, however.

Documented Rough Draft Report

At least three campaign irregularities have been traced to the organization in California.

The first campaign was the mayoral race. The candidate's committee filed false reports of expenditures with both city and state governments.

The second campaign was the mayoral run-off election a month later. The organization sponsored an effort to oppose the incumbant mayor. In its own journal, the group said that 50,000 fliers had been distributed in this effort. No report, however, was filed with either city or state officials as was required by law.

The third campaign law violation occurred in the presidential race. Although the organization made expenditures in the state on behalf of the candidate, it failed to report them to the Secretary of State as is required by Federal Elections law.

--30--

135

Index of Documents

Lines 1 & 2	Explained and documented in paragraphs 3, 4, and 5
Line 3	Exhibit A, statement of committee, Dolbeare for Mayor
Lines 4,5	Exhibit B-1, affidavits of two printers named in expenditures, exhibit A B-1, B-2, see exhibit A page 1, stamps of city clerk and state attorney general
Line 6	Exhibit C, flier, "Citizens for San Francisco"
Line 8	Exhibit D, notes of interviews confirming that both New Solidarity and Executive Intelligence Journal are organs of the U.S. Labor Party, or "the organization," apparently the National Caucus of Labor Committees. Also see exhibit D-2 documenting ties between the publications and the organizations
Line 9	Exhibits E-1, E-2, clippings, NewS. & EIR
Lines 10, 11	Exhibits F-1, F-2, notes from calls to city clerk and Secretary of State
Line 11	Exhibit G-1, G-2, copies city and state election statutes
Lines 13, 14	Exhibit H-1, H-2, H-3, notes of fund-raising event; campaign flier listing addresses and phones in state; notes of phone calls to these offices
Line 14	Exhibit I, notes, call to Secretary of State
Line 15	Exhibit J, copy FEC laws as amended.

Edited Report

Three political campaigns linked to the U.S. Labor Party/National Caucus of Labor Committees (USLP/NCLC) during the last half of 1979 apparently violated city, state, or federal elections laws.

In June, Patricia Dolbeare, a member of the USLP/NCLC executive committee and Northern California coordinator of the Citizens for LaRouche presidential campaign, announced that she was running for mayor of San Francisco. In what was apparently the first flier of the campaign, Dolbeare said she was running "in tandem with the 1980 presidential campaign of Lyndon LaRouche, national chairman of the U.S. Labor Party." Copies of the campaign committee's termination report on file with both the city clerk and the secretary of state say that the campaign committee spent $1,722, of which $1,256 was spent for the filing fee and $466 was spent on printing and other unitemized expenditures. The committee reported that it used two printers, claiming a single $131 expense at one shop. An owner of the print shop estimated that the campaign spent "at least $500" in his shop, that the shop "never" did "any" press run for the campaign that cost $131, and found a copy of one of the receipts for campaign fliers for a print run that cost $185. No such expense was listed on the committee's reports. The treasurer of the committee was unavailable for comment about the apparent discrepancies between the print-shop records and the campaign committee's filings.

A week before the mayoral campaign, Citizens for Dolbeare had apparently either moved without a forwarding phone number, or had dissolved. Dolbeare's personal phone number, however, had a new listing.

A few days before the run-off election campaign about one month later, a new committee emerged, called "Citizens for San Francisco". It apparently issued only one flier. The phone number listed on the flier was identical to Dolbeare's, and the committee was apparently a reincarnation of Dolbeare's mayoral race.

Two USLP/NCLC-linked publications reported that the committee, allegedly "non-partisan", had distributed 50,000 copies of the flier. Political committees receiving or spending in excess of $500 to influence local elections are required to file financial statements with the city and, in some instances, with the state. Estimates from local printers for a 50,000 press run were in excess of $500, but no record of this committee could be found either in city or state offices under this name.

Federal law, meanwhile, requires that every organization for a presidential candidate report its expenditures to the state. Despite what would appear to be expenditures by Citizens for LaRouche during the last half of 1979 for office space in Los Angeles and San Francisco, telephones, campaign literature, and expenses related to at least two benefits for the campaign, Citizens for LaRouche had apparently made no filings in California as of the end of February 1980, one month after the 1979 filing deadline.

-30-

Analysis

The edited report is nearly three times longer than the rough draft report. The main reason for this is that the rough draft report is primarily made up of conclusions based on presumed facts. The edited report gets rid of a lot of the conclusions and purges most of the presumptions from the rough draft.

Paragraph One:

"at least three" changed to "three"

The original led to the presumption that there were other campaigns but that nothing was wrong with them, a situation the investigator knew nothing about. The change limits the report to the things the investigator is aware of.

"irregularities" changed to "apparently violated city, state, or federal elections laws"

The original "irregularities" did not necessarily mean there were any legal violations. Note the word "apparent" before violations. This protects deniability in case the report overlooked something that would mean that there wasn't any violation.

"traced to the org." changed to "linked to"

No evidence was found that NCLC/USLP directly controlled these campaigns. Note: documentation of these links must be added to the documentation package. Evidence includes: (1) internal reports that all money raised by NCLC/USLP is daily sent to New York headquarters where it is apparently managed by NCLC/USLP leaders; and (2) documentation of Dolbeare's role in the group, including various notes showing that all addresses tied to the three California campaigns were used simultaneously for NSIPS, CFL, NCLC and other related groups.

Paragraph Two:

The entire paragraph has been changed to accomplish these goals: (1) in the rough draft the words "the first campaign" were vague; (2) the evidence of Dolbeare's ties with the parent groups are presented up front so the reader isn't left with too many questions about how the investigator came to believe the ties between organizations were genuine; (3) note the word "apparently" in reference to the first flier -- the investigator could not be sure that there weren't others before that; (4) the flier is quoted because the campaigns "in tandem" lend credence to the argument that the mayoral campaign was merely an extension of the presidential campaign; (5) rather than have the investigator say that the reports are false, the investigator reports what was learned -- therefore, the details of expenses, printer's statements, etc. are given. This again protects "deniability" in the event that accurate reports were filed and then lost by city and state officials; (6)

since it is basically the printer's word against the committee's reports, it was necessary to try to get the treasurer to explain the inconsistencies. The treasurer had moved and no phone listing was available at the time the investigator completed this phase of the investigation.

Paragraph Three:

This paragraph has also been completely changed, and in the edited version, becomes paragraphs three, four, and five. New paragraph three shows part of the tie between the mayoral race and the second campaign. The tie is Dolbeare's phone number, as is elaborated in new paragraph four. In paragraphs three and four of the edited report, note the "apparently" qualifiers. They are there because the investigator is making conclusions based on facts. As in paragraph two, new paragraph five gives the actual details learned by the investigator. Note the last sentence of new paragraph five, "no record...could be found...under this name." This allows for the possibility that the committee filed under a different name not known to the investigator.

Paragraph Four:

"third...violation" changed to (no mention of time or numerical order of apparent violation because what is being described may in fact have been a continuous process of violations.

"violation occurred" changed to (description of facts as investigator found them).

"failed to report" changed to "Citizens for LaRouche had apparently made no filings..."

As before, filings can get lost. Also, it's been known to happen that about three hours after a report is made and before it is distributed, subjects suddenly decide to make legally required filings. Giving the date the investigator checked allows for the possibility of a late filing while covering the investigator's credibility. Then, if the group filed on March 1, the investigator could report that, **and***, the original report would stand uncompromised.*

General Comments

I recommend spelling out the details of investigations as much as possible for two reasons: *(1)* it adds to the investigator's credibility because the person who reads the report will know on what data the report is based; and *(2)* it allows an independent investigator to repeat the findings which again adds to credibility.

Interestingly, after this report was made, a campaign worker for Citizens For LaRouche pooh-pooed the report saying, "they must have really had to scratch the bottom of the barrell if *all* they could find was (a) $500 (violation)." It is a point well-taken, except that even such minor violations can have serious affects. Under some circumstances, violations of the federal elections laws can be a felony, which can include not only a heavy fine, but a prison sentence of up to five years in duration as well. Violations of the state and local elections codes are misdemeanors. Additionally, civil suits can be brought that will result in the candidate or committee having to pay back to donors and to the state certain fines and assessments. Violations of the federal law that are made by presidential candidates who have received federal matching funds may mean not only that further funds will be denied, but that the candidate may have to return the matching funds already received. Unfortunately, election laws are seldom enforced equally. A violation that might cause havoc for the LaRouche campaign might be overlooked if it were done by the Carter campaign. In some cases, massive violations may be found, and no enforcement official will try to enforce the laws for fear of alienating powerful political leaders.

It is interesting to contrast the approach used in this sample report with a report appearing in the *New York Times*. Reporters there, it was said, had tried to prove that the NCLC/USLP had ties to the CIA -- a great story had it been true. Apparently as a result of following this direction, the final *NYT* report included no mention of or proof of, any allegedly illegal activities.

The investigator following Harry's Fourth Law will know which report had the most effect, the much-ballyhooed *NYT* piece, or the little report about apparently tiny election law violations...

APPENDIX 3
THE CITIZEN INVESTIGATOR'S LIBRARY

Every good investigator keeps a list of all the sources and contacts he or she has made over the years. These contacts and sources come in handy at surprising times. If an investigator is involved in an intense project that focuses on certain types of illegal acts: e.g., Securities and Exchange Commission fraud, the investigator will do well to get copies of the relevant state and federal laws and keep them handy. Reviewing the law can help you recognize an illegal act when you see one.

Some investigators keep their offices equipped with cross-reference directories, phone books, and *Who's Whos* of the region. Aside from phone books I do not keep many books around. I let my computer do the searching. It saves time and space.

Here's a list of the materials that I have found valuable enough to keep around with some comments about them:

Advanced Investigative Techniques for Private Financial Records, by Richard A. Nossen. Loompanics Unlimited, 1983.

Although most of the records described in this handy book are private, it's not uncommon for an investigator to run across some of this material either from sources, accidentally, or even in the public domain. Some corporation files, for example, contain correspondence that includes copies of cancelled checks to show proof that fees were paid. It's a good idea to know how to get as much information as you can from a check and Nossen's material shows you how you can do so. The Nossen book also is an excellent introduction to a style and consciousness of investigating that the citizen investigator should be familiar with: how to follow a financial trail and, more importantly, how to put the pieces of the puzzle together to create an entire picture.

Citizen Investigator's Checklist. 1984, Lewis & Clarke Explorations.

An essential guide for the citizen investigator, it's yours free when you send a self-addressed, stamped envelope. An invaluable chart of where to look for documents on people, business, and politics in federal, state and local records. An essential guide for the citizen investigator. Send your SASE to Lewis & Clarke, PO Box 32878, San Jose, CA 95152.

Data Bases for Business; Profiles and Applications, by Van Mayros and D. Michael Warner. Chilton, 1982.

Definitely oriented to business, but it does list most of the electronic data bases and vendors you'll probably use. I like this directory because it gives some useful information on developing search strategies and finding cost effective ways of developing information.

Finding Facts Fast: How to Find Out What You Want and Need To Know, by Alden Todd. William Morrow & Co., 1972. Ten Speed Press, 1979.

As a general guide to public data, including a good list of the different types of directories that are published, this is handy to have around. It's a classic and so it's a bit outdated.

How to Use the Freedom of Information Act (FOIA), by L.G. Sherick. Arco Publishing Comapny, Inc., 1978.

Changes imposed during the Reagan administration have made the FOIA incredibly difficult and expensive for the citizen investigator to use, so this book is a bit outdated. Still, it's the best book (and the best set of laws for citizen investigators) around.

Legal Research: How to Find and Understand the Law, by Stephen Elias. 1982. Nolo Press, 950 Parker St., Berkeley, CA 94710.

Absolutely the best reference on the subject. Even though material on electronic data bases is slim, the information is easily transferred to your computer search. Nolo Press is a super resource on many legal issues. People who are on their mailing list (send a $5.00 "voluntary subscription") get invaluable updates on the self-help law movement.

National Directory of Addresses and Telephone Numbers; 1980-81 Edition. Bantam Books, 1979.

Among the most useful things I use are the numbers of newspapers in various parts of the country. Much of the material is outdated, but if you can find a copy it's probably worth your money.

Plugging In: A Guide to the World of Telecommunications for the Microcomputerist, by Sasha Lewis. Chilton, 1984.

Another winner from Chilton. The best resource for the citizen investigator who wants to extend his or her computer system into the expanding universe of electronic research.

Raising Hell: A Citizens Guide to the Fine Art of Investigation, by Dan Noys. Updated, published by *Mother Jones* magazine.

If you can get a copy (it was originally free), you'll find an incredible wealth of information on how to use public documents in its 32 pages. The pamphlet also has a useful bibliography (even though it doesn't mention this book).

The Writer's Resource Guide, edited by Bernadine Clark. Writers Digest Books, 1983.

An indispensable general reference to contacts in various organizations and libraries.

The World Connection, by Timothy Orr Knight. Howard W. Sams & Co., 1983.

If you're thinking of buying a computer to help in your research, this book should help you decide if it's worth the trouble or not. Introductory material but useful and easy to understand.

Where's What: Sources of Information for Federal Investigators, by Harry J. Murphy, Office of Security, Central Intelligence Agency. Warner Books, 1976.

Let's hope this book is always available somewhere. Originally a CIA manual it is the super-reference on who has you on file where. Most of the information it lists isn't legally avaiable to the citizen investigator, but it's handy to know what's out there in case you ever need it.

APPENDIX 4
A NOTE FROM THE AUTHOR

Three years after the first edition of this book was published, I got a call from a source I used in an article I published that was very similar to the example in Appendix 2. The source had received a $50,000 judgment for libel in federal court. It's rare that the citizen investigator actually sees positive results from his or her work (he or she may move, lose interest in the subject, or generally become discouraged), so I was especially pleased by the call. The delay between publication and the phone call was four years. That's about average.

So let's initiate *Harry's 19th Law:* **Right Wins Out...In the End** Have faith in that; maintain your integrity, and you'll get the satisfaction of knowing that not only have you helped an individual or two, but you have helped to create social change.

Meanwhile, if you would like a little help from a friend, you can contact me through Lewis & Clarke Explorations, P.O. Box 32878, San Jose, CA 95152. I'm available for a fee (negotiable) through this information brokerage.

Good hunting in your investigations. May the good guys always win.

— **M. Harry**

YOU WILL ALSO WANT TO READ:

- ☐ **ADVANCED INVESTIGATIVE TECHNIQUES FOR PRIVATE FINANCIAL RECORDS, by Richard A. Nossen.**

    This manual reveals the *exact* methods used by government agents to snoop into *your* private financial records! Contents include: Checking and savings accounts; Safe deposit boxes; Bank loan files; Cashiers and travelers checks; Foreign bank accounts; Brokerage accounts; Credit card records; Real property records; And much more! *Everything* about your most private transactions can be learned *without your even being told you're under investigation!* Find out how. Order your copy today! *1983, Large 8½ x 11, 86 pp, illustrated, soft cover. $10.00.* (Order Number 13032)

- ☐ **COVERT SURVEILLANCE & ELECTRONIC PENETRATION, edited by William B. Moran.**

    A how-to-do-it manual for government agents, this book details professional techniques for spying and eavesdropping. Topics covered include: Shadowing and tailing; Fixed and mobile surveillance; Vehicle surveillance; Night vision devices; Electronic eavesdropping devices; Body-mounted transmitters; Concealed microphones; Wiretapping; Interception of computer data; Telephone bugging; and much more! *Is Big Brother watching you?* You bet he is, and this book tells you *exactly* how he's doing it! *1983, Large 8½ x 11, 51 pp, illustrated, soft cover. $6.95.* (Order Number 55043)

- ☐ **WIRETAPPING AND ELECTRONIC SURVEILLANCE: Commission Studies.**

    A gold mine of practical information relating to the nuts and bolts of wiretapping and bugging! Topics covered include: Audio eavesdropping; Telephone wiretapping; Telephone room eavesdropping; Infinity transmitters; Special purpose microphones; Radio eavesdropping devices; Wireless microphone transmitters; Miniature devices; Microwave devices; Tape recording systems; Tracking systems; And much more! Contains suprisingly thorough, *illustrated* descriptions of a wide variety of state-of-the-art electronic surveillance techniques and equipment. *1976, Large 8½ x 11, 112 pp, profusely illustrated, soft cover. $9.95.* (Order Number 58021)

And mcuh more! We offer the very finest in controversial and unusual books — please turn to the catalog announcement on the next page!

Loompanics Unlimited   PO Box 1197   Pt Townsend, WA 98368

Please send me the books I have checked above. I am enclosing $_____
(please include $1.00 per book for shipping and handling—if ordering 3 or more, only $2.00 is necessary).

Name _____

Address_____ Apt. No._____

City_____ State_____ Zip_____

We use UPS delivery (unless otherwise requested) if you give us a street address.   MM

CONTROVERSIAL AND UNUSUAL BOOKS!!!

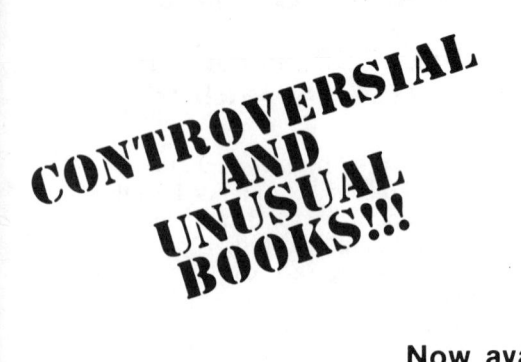

"Yes, there are books about the skills of apocalypse -- spying, surveillance, fraud, wire-tapping, smuggling, self-defense, lockpicking, gunmanship, eavesdropping, car chasing, civil warfare, surviving jail, and dropping out of sight. Apparently writing books is the way mercenaries bring in spare cash between wars. The books are useful, and it's good the information is freely available (and they definitely inspire interesting dreams), but their advice should be taken with a salt shaker or two and a by your wits. A few of these volumes are truly scary. Loompanics is the best of the Libertarian suppliers who carry them. Though full of 'you'll-wish-you'd-read-these-when-it's-too-late' rhetoric, their catalog is genuinely informative."

-THE NEXT WHOLE EARTH CATALOG

Now available:
THE BEST BOOK CATALOG IN THE WORLD!!!

- Large 8½ x 11 size!
- More than 500 of the most controversial and unusual books ever printed!!!
- YOU can order EVERY book listed!!!
- Periodic Supplements to keep you posted on the LATEST titles available!!!

We offer hard-to-find books on the world's most unusual subjects. Here are a few of the topics covered IN DEPTH in our exciting new catalog:

- *Hiding/concealment of physical objects!* A complete section of the best books ever written on hiding things!
- *Fake ID/Alternate Identities!* The most comprehensive selection of books on this little-known subject ever offered for sale! You have to see it to believe it!
- *Investigative/Undercover methods and techniques!* Professional secrets known only to a few, now revealed for YOU to use! Actual police manuals on shadowing and surveillance!
- *And much, much more, including Locks and Locksmithing, Self Defense, Intelligence Increase, Life Extension, Money-Making Opportunities,* and much, much more!

Our book catalog is truly THE BEST BOOK CATALOG IN THE WORLD! Order yours today -- you will be very pleased, we know.

(Our catalog is free with the order of any book on the previous page -- or is $2.00 if ordered by itself.)

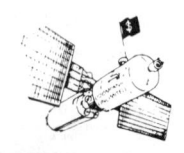

Loompanics Unlimited
PO Box 1197
Pt Townsend, WA 98368
USA